VISIONS OF HOME

VISIONS OF HOME

TIMELESS DESIGN, MODERN SENSIBILITY

ANDREW COGAR
and Partners of HISTORICAL CONCEPTS

Written with Marc Kristal
Photography by Eric Piasecki

RIZZOLI
NEW YORK

New York · Paris · London · Milan

CONTENTS

WHAT'S IN A NAME?
VISION AS REFLECTION

When our first book, *Coming Home*, was published in 2012, it represented more than a catalogue of the firm's work up to that point. It was a celebration of our belief, as I wrote, in "the warmth and charm that lies at the heart of Southern architecture." But it was also a celebration of a dream I'd held close to my heart since childhood.

Atlanta was a sleepy town when I was growing up, and Buckhead, where we lived, was a little community. Yet to my young eyes, there were wonders on display. Riding my bicycle down Valley Road to go fishing or heading to school on the bus, I'd pass magnificent residences dating from the interwar years, designed by the legends of Southern classical architecture. Captivated by these mansions, the creations of Neel Reid, Philip Shutze, Lewis Crook, and others, I couldn't say why I so admired them—back then, I lacked the language. But I knew they were good. And I knew as well that, someday, I wanted to design houses that were the equal of those around me.

"Someday" arrived in 1982, when Historical Concepts opened its doors. At that time, almost no one was designing or building traditional residences, and remarkably, classical architecture wasn't being dependably taught in the schools. But this only made my passion burn hotter. I knew that I wanted to—no, *had* to—create a firm with a design philosophy based on classical traditions and local precedent. So, I undertook the journey, and as things turned out, many people shared my passion. Over time, Historical Concepts created a broad portfolio of homes, drawing on the rich traditions of Southern classicism, in Atlanta and across the Southeast. *Coming Home* is a record of that dream come true, a dream shared equally with my partners and associates.

Today, though our philosophy remains the same, Historical Concepts is a larger, more forward-looking version of what it was when that first book was published. I am particularly proud of our working method, which extends our passion for architectural precedent into the realm of narrative. Many historic houses evolved over time, as the circumstances of their owners improved, or the properties changed hands, becoming an amalgam of parts that together relate a tale of change and evolution—personal, stylistic, and regional. When we design a new home, we also attempt to tell a story, but one constructed from the emotions, tastes, and needs of the individuals or families that the home will serve. It is immensely satisfying to share with clients our research into architectural precedents: to see their responses from the perspectives of both emotion and logic, and to understand what drives those responses. These become the basis of our narrative, at once historical and contemporary, regional and personal.

Architects often speak about context, which is to say, a home's relationship to its natural and built environments, its specific moment in time and place in

PAGES 2–3, 4, 6, AND 8: Situated on the pristine shores of Spring Island, South Carolina, this home takes full advantage of its peninsular setting, with water views framed by live oaks and loblolly pines. The stately Greek Revival cottage is supported by a series of ancillary buildings, each making its own detailed additions to the architectural language (see page 8).

a community. All of this matters to us a great deal, but it's our clients that remain the most critical part of the context for any project. Their hopes, dreams, and needs are our primary source of inspiration and the touchstone by which we measure our success. Consequently, we tend to shy away from working with folks who say, "Do something grand and call me when it's finished." It is the human element—the sparks of joy and creativity that arise from client interaction—that puts a skip in our step and gives purpose and meaning to our work.

Given all this, I'm often asked why a firm with such a personal philosophy and approach has such an impersonal name. Why Historical Concepts instead of, for example, James L. Strickland Architects? Fair enough. I chose our name for two reasons. The first was that our animating idea was the creation of contemporary homes rooted in the timeless values of history, and I wanted potential clients to understand this the moment they heard our name. The second, more important reason had to do with my long-standing interest in the people with whom I work: my sincere belief that everything I am derives from my associates. I always believed that I was designing, not just houses, but a philosophy of practice—one based on the quality and character of the individuals around me—and that, if the firm wasn't *about* me, it could have a life *beyond* me. When I leaf through

Coming Home today, those individuals are what I see first. And I believe this spirit reflects the humility with which we approach each project. The result is an architecture that pays homage to the traditions that inspired it, and to the clients who entrust us with their dreams.

Finding a successor to guide the firm forward as a steward of these beliefs meant something very personal to me. And so I am immensely grateful to have discovered a kindred spirit in Andrew Cogar, the author of this book, and the individual who'll lead Historical Concepts into its next phase as an architecture and planning firm. In our office, we've spent considerable time articulating our personal and collective values, two of which remain particularly appropriate to Andrew's approach. The first is that every design is an opportunity to create something special. The second is that design should be about context and precedent and not ego and individualism. These values, as a call to action, set the tone for our future work, and provide me with the confidence that there will be a clear line of continuity between what was, and what is to come.

I am proud of what I've achieved alongside everyone with whom I've worked. But beginnings are footnotes. On the pages that follow you will see what the future has in store—and discover, truly, what there is in a name.

—James L. Strickland

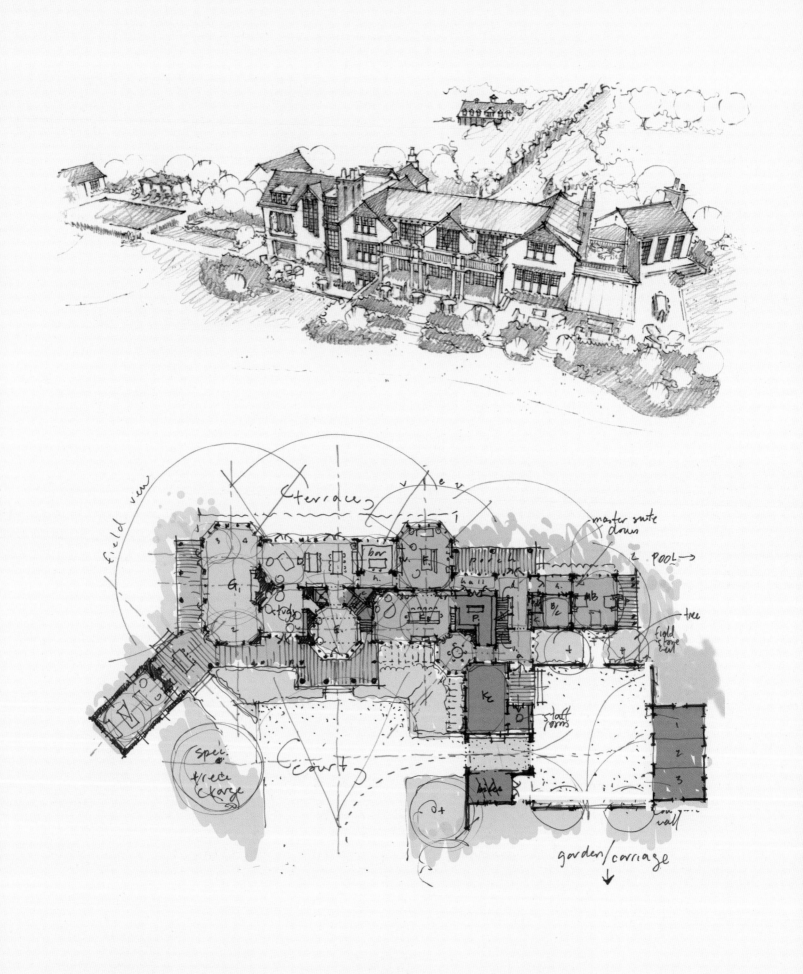

STORYTELLING
VISION AS MEMORY

Wen we look around our homes, what do we see? Furniture and photographs, family heirlooms and sentimental keepsakes. But the things we perceive most vividly—those that invest a home with real value and purpose—aren't visible to the naked eye. These are memories. The kids' first steps. Glasses raised to birthdays and anniversaries. A thousand good mornings and as many good nights. Homes are where we create, and immerse ourselves in, personal history. And the longer we live in them, the more layered and evocative our memories become, until, eventually, an act as simple and casual as crossing a room can bring forth a wellspring of emotions: recollections and experiences we can't see but are very much *there*, ever-present and deeply felt.

Certainly this has been the case for me. Growing up, my family moved multiple times, to a variety of places, and many of my earliest memories are framed by domestic architecture. Indeed, at family gatherings, our past homes serve as central characters in the stories we tell: that cherished window seat, perfect for curling up and reading on a winter's day; the loft overlooking the living room, ideal for launching toy paratroopers at guests below; a first-floor window that could be jimmied open when we slipped in past curfew. Each event, in its own special setting, has become an indelible part of our family's collective narrative. And that has profoundly influenced how I think about what I do. The architect has many tasks to consider when designing a home. But none is as important as creating a place that will encourage the making, and keeping, of memories.

One of the best ways to do this, we've found, is to construct a house around a story. Creating a narrative—as important to architecture as it is to literature or film—transforms a building from a collection of rooms into a place animated by a way of life, one informed by dreams. Yet, while you'd think that helping people realize their most cherished desires would be easy, persuading clients to open their hearts and reveal what "home" means to them can be quite challenging. In a way, it's not surprising. Perhaps most of us are more comfortable expressing our stylistic preferences and everyday needs than articulating our strongest emotions and dreams.

Therein lies the magic of inspired storytelling. Creating a historical narrative lets you tell the truth about how you really want to live without feeling awkward or self-conscious. That narrative also provokes the personal revelations and moments of clarity that are so valuable to how we work. If you've always fancied living in a Colonial-era farmstead, let's say, it can be much easier—and more creative—to dream up what life might have been like for previous generations than to project yourself into an as yet unbuilt house. We can then translate those fantasies into a concrete plan and a built reality. And because the story you're inventing is your own, you start making memories not just on move-in day, but from the first moment we collaborate on the design.

The two projects that follow—one in the South Carolina Lowcountry, the other nestled in Sun Valley, Idaho—could not be more different in appearance or regional spirit. Yet both homes arose from the clients' embrace of historical narrative, and enthusiasm for writing "stories" for their homes that were entwined with the lives they dreamed of living. As you'll see, it's a wonderful way to bring a design to life—and to make it indelibly your own.

PAGES 10, 11, AND ABOVE: Preliminary sketches allow us to engage with our clients from the very start of the design process. Drawings like these enable homeowners to visualize our architectural ideas and become co-authors of their own stories.

Natural History

Architects often start with a blank slate and let their imaginations roam freely. Yet homes that incorporate parts of earlier structures, or sit upon storied properties with a past, require a heightened sensitivity and awareness. This idea informed the design of a residence in the South Carolina Lowcountry, on an 1,800-acre property with a complex social, agrarian, and architectural legacy.

Presently a tree farm and hunting preserve, the land's rice ponds, built with slave labor, reflect its origins as a grant from the English Crown. Inhabited in the late 1600s, according to local lore the main house was burned three times—first by the Indigenous Coosa tribe, then the British during the Revolution, and finally by the Union Army after 1861. Dotted with outbuildings from different centuries, lush with live oak and loblolly pine and combed by river breezes, the property's history was so tangled, so turbulent, that it seemed the very embodiment of William Faulkner's famous observation: "The past is never dead. It's not even past."

Yet the absence of a single dominant period freed us from feeling beholden to a particular architectural moment. And we were supported by our clients, whose interests lay in respecting the past without idealizing it. They wanted a home that expressed their passions for history, modern art, land conservation, big-game hunting, and exotic collectibles. The outcome is a house that employs the premise of generational additions and adaptive reuse to layer multiple moments of invented history: a design that lets the house be "classical" while embracing a contemporary way of life, framed by decoration at once quietly elegant and playfully eccentric.

The project confirms the maxim that limitations are often the best generators of inspiration. Architecturally, the style combines elements of nineteenth-century Greek Revival with the artisanal quirks and details found in Charleston and the Lowcountry. While not specifically indebted to Palladio, the house captures the simple beauty of his renowned villas: on the one hand, boldly axial, spatially generous, and grand in gesture; on the other, pragmatic, unpretentious, and comfortable. What gives the design its special distinction, however, is our creative answer to the square-footage limitations our clients embraced to help protect the land. In response to these constraints, we broke the house into three components, arranged around a front ornamental boxwood garden. The result is a whole composed of parts, each of which enjoys its own particular narrative.

The story involved a grand main pavilion that might have been erected in the early 1800s, with a century's worth of subsequent alterations to the secondary buildings. We imagined three or four generations, each of which made changes to incorporate the modern conveniences of their day. With our clients' participation, the evolution of each component became quite specific. The wing housing the owners' suite we considered to have been two freestanding structures—a kitchen and a laundry—converted into, respectively, a bedroom and dressing room. These structures were then connected sometime in the early twentieth century by a quietly glamorous, glass-enclosed bath. Directly across the front garden we placed the guest wing, conceived as an eighteenth-century carriage house, its two stalls transformed into bedrooms with ensuite baths, and a

PREVIOUS SPREAD: The three pavilions that collectively comprise this Lowcountry residence occupy a landscaped precinct within sight of the property's original rice pond dykes. OPPOSITE: Beneath the delicate fretwork of the roof parapet, the main pavilion's strongly articulated Greek Doric entry portico is a nod to the regional architecture prevalent in the early nineteenth century.

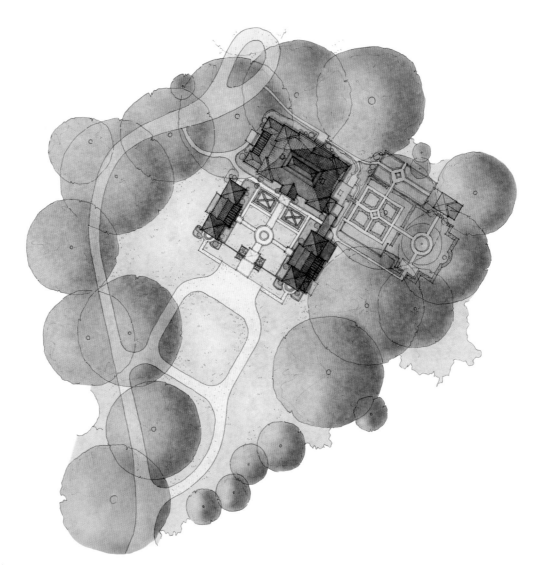

cozy entry hall in the middle. The matching structures, capped by zinc-clad pyramidal roofs, convey a stately unity while framing the front entry to the home, and together unite the overall composition.

The main pavilion features a formal Greek Doric entry portico, a gesture typical of the region's early nineteenth-century buildings. But it's the interior that delivers the big surprise. Set between long axial enfilades on the building's north and south sides is a 45-by-25-foot great hall, which, with its multitude of trophy mounts and wildlife tableaux, feels like a domestic version of a natural history gallery. The room's soaring verticality and exposed rough-hewn beams give the space airiness, natural light, and, not least, drama.

Our clients, tireless collectors of things serious and whimsical, crafted the very lively interiors with designer Barbara Westbrook, filling the rooms with curiosities that start—and stop—conversation. It came as no surprise when we discovered their admiration for Teddy Roosevelt. That energetic adventurer and storyteller extraordinaire would feel entirely at ease here, in a home inspired in equal measure by conservation, creativity, and hospitality.

ABOVE: The house sits at the end of a long and winding road, culminating in a motor court and formal front garden. OPPOSITE: The two bedroom wings, one containing the owners' suite, the other a pair of guest rooms, share restrained yet elegant brick detailing and pyramid-shaped, hand-crimped zinc roofs.

LEFT: The abundant landscaping interweaves new work by Don Hooten with earlier landscape elements, the oldest—the Parterre Garden—dating from 1703. FOLLOWING SPREAD: Steel-framed windows and doors behind the Greek Doric columns enclose the water-facing veranda (called the "story-telling room") and suggest a twentieth-century intervention.

PAGE 24: The new architecture and landscape (TOP LEFT AND RIGHT) take their cues from the existing historic walled gardens and brick ancillary structures (BOTTOM LEFT AND RIGHT) with special attention and care given to proportions and detailing. PAGE 25: The house's water-facing orientation lets the library, "storytelling room," and dining room capture the glow of the setting Lowcountry sun.

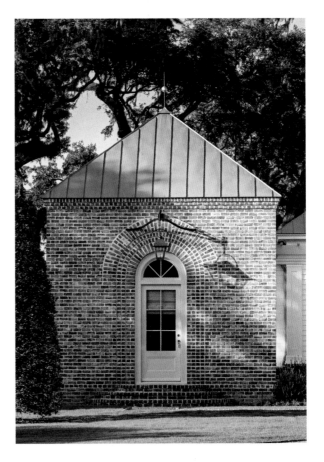

PAGES 26 AND 27: A covered walkway connects the pavilions, the brickwork paths extending to an outdoor seating area. ABOVE AND OPPOSITE: Beyond the front entry lies the great hall, a domestic version of a natural history gallery, displaying a diverse collection of wildlife tableaux and artworks, including original Audubon prints. Primarily an entertainment space, the room's custom-pigmented plaster walls are warmed by heart pine-wainscoting and antique hand-hewn beams, which also serve to domesticate the grand scale.

PAGES 30 AND 31: The library (LEFT), paneled in cypress reclaimed from the nearby waters, faces the casual, welcoming "storytelling room" (RIGHT) and, beyond it, the informal dining space off the kitchen.
ABOVE: The circular west gallery—which connects the entry hall, kitchen, and mudroom—features curved cabinets showcasing the wife's collections. OPPOSITE: The loblolly pine beams (harvested on the property), along with the robust island, express the kitchen's rustic charm.

ABOVE: The paneled wall and half-round window behind the bed in the owners' bedroom suggest an arched door to a former horse stall that had been closed up when the barn was converted to sleeping quarters.
OPPOSITE: Above the bedroom's fireplace, a striking illuminated "infinity butterfly mirror" by artist Jocelyn Marsh provides a whimsical counterpoint to the rustic hearth and vintage chairs.

ABOVE AND RIGHT: In the fictional timeline we constructed for the house, the glamorous bath, which looks across the forecourt garden to the guest wing, was added in the early twentieth century. This narrative allowed us to insert a glass wall at the tub, which opens onto an outdoor shower.

Rather than approaching the house via a straight road leading to the front door, we softened the arrival experience, bending the drive around a majestic old live oak, which serves as a sentinel at the front of the residence.

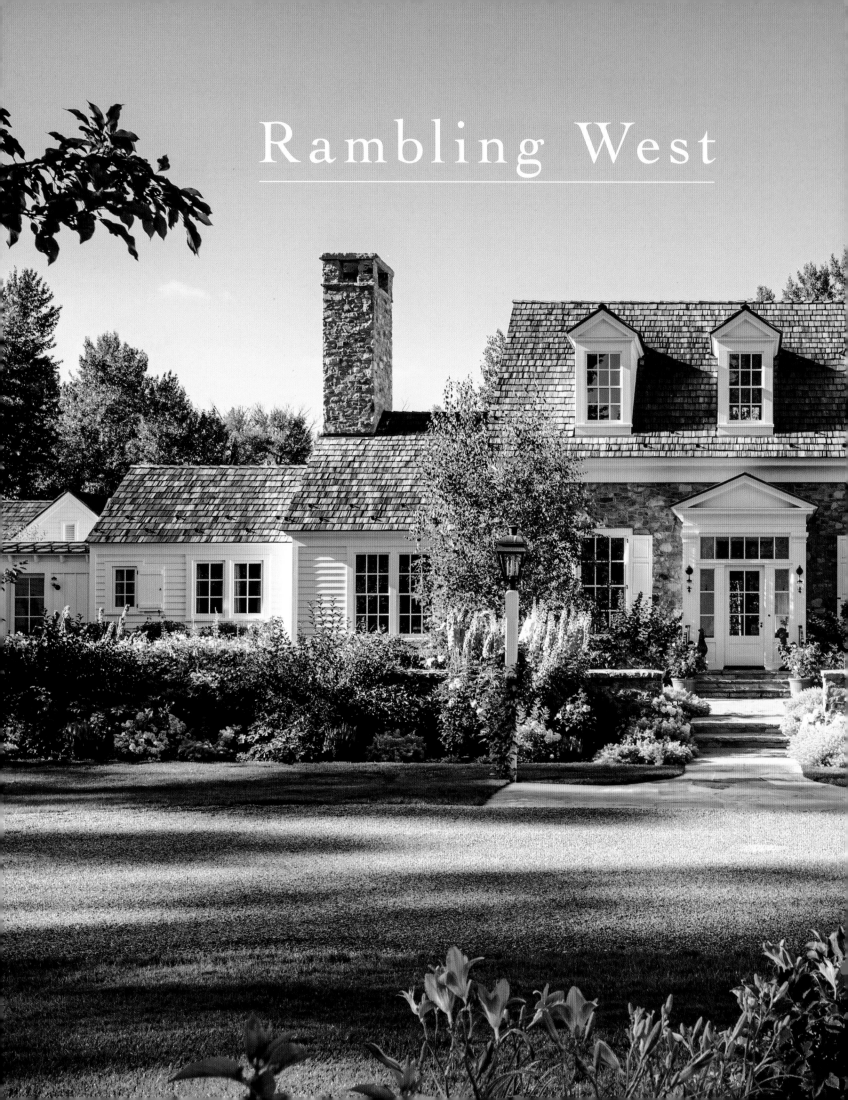

Rambling West

There is a special pleasure to be had from working with a client more than once. The more you understand how someone thinks and feels, the better able you are to distill that into the essence of home. Most important, an ongoing collaboration lets everyone get to know, and trust, one another—not just professionally, but personally.

Starting off in California, these particular clients had lived in New England, South Carolina, and Montana before alighting in this majestic Idaho landscape. The house, located in the Wood River Valley between Hailey and Sun Valley, was the sixth project the firm undertook for the couple; here, they wanted to bring a bit of every place they'd lived and loved, while also embracing Sun Valley's historical roots.

The big challenge involved combining aspects of all those previous homes (and their varying regional influences) into a residence that was aesthetically authentic to Sun Valley and connected to the site. Immersing ourselves in research, we made a fortuitous discovery: when this part of the West was being developed, the domestic architecture was, in fact, directly related to the construction methods prevalent in New England at that time. Further exploring history, we became intrigued by the idea of the evolving homestead. Typically, settlers would construct a main house supported by several outbuildings, often a cookhouse, carriage barn, and wellhead. Then subsequent generations would fill in the spaces between, connecting the various structures as their needs changed and fortunes fluctuated. The outcome would be a rambling house, revealing different layers of scale, style, and material.

This approach presented several advantages. It allowed us to unite the wide variety of architectural elements favored by our clients. Adding open and enclosed porches let us soften the border between structure and nature and enable the residents to better enjoy their patch of paradise. The rambling arrangement also meant that we could build a big house that wouldn't be overwhelming—one that nestled into the land rather than imposing on it. Thus, we proposed a residence driven by a narrative of multigenerational evolution, a story embracing stone, clapboard, and board-and-batten, porches and breezeways—a house the very cohesion of which arose from its diversity. The clients approved at once, and enthusiastically participated in the creation of this architectural tale.

The building's core is a story-and-a-half Greek Revival farmhouse. Simple and efficient, this is historically the sort of first step a homesteader would have chosen to build. Telescoping off this stone-clad structure in both directions are more modest clapboard wings that descend in size. One contains the rustic kitchen and keeping room (a Colonial-era space, adjacent to the kitchen, used for informal dining and gatherings). The other holds his-and-hers offices and an exercise room, also clad in stone (the imagined original cookhouse). These two wings, in our story, went up simultaneously as second-generation additions accommodating a growing family in need of space. The owners' suite, also built of stone both inside and out, we imagined as an original outbuilding (a dairy or stable). On the house's far-off other wing, a gabled extension—perhaps once an icehouse or smokehouse—serves as guest quarters.

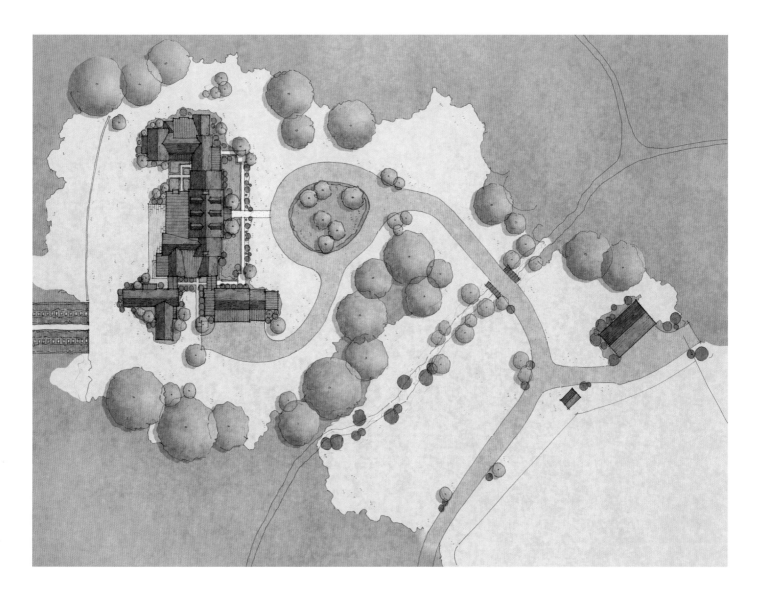

It sounds simple, but there's a hidden challenge in a rambling plan: developing effective, interesting interstitial spaces. A favorite example arose from the wife's request for an office with both front and rear views. In the plan, the back of her space abutted a hallway. Accordingly, we added a small bay to the hall for a windowed sitting nook and then inserted internal windows between it and her office—thereby creating a direct visual connection from the office to the lush rear gardens. Quiet, subtle transitions like these softened and concealed the building's true scale (measuring 100 feet end to end) and generated some of the most memorable vignettes.

As we built the story beat by beat, we realized that many of the principles that applied to the house were not far from what they would have been 150 years ago—the past and present narratives were, in effect, one and the same. This unity is the reason that a place that makes a virtue of diversity appears so cohesive. So it's no accident that this most rambling of homes looks like it happened naturally, intentionally, and almost inevitably over time.

OPPOSITE: This quaint porch is a favorite meeting spot for the husband-and-wife homeowners, connecting both her office (to the left) and his office (straight ahead). ABOVE: The site plan reveals the house's well-disguised scale and rambling character.

ABOVE: A bank of windows bathes the keeping room in natural daylight. OPPOSITE: Beyond the cold room, the house opens up to a one-and-a-half-story great room that combines formal living and dining.

Reclaimed wide-plank floors and a wood ceiling infuse the kitchen with warmth. Cabinetry is tucked beneath the windows to preserve natural light and views. Opposite the brick pizza oven to the left, and styled to resemble part of the room's cabinetry, is the refrigerator.

ABOVE AND OPPOSITE: Decorative artist Martine Drackett painted a pastoral mural on panels, which are suspended from an iron track. The panels can be drawn to separate the kitchen from the keeping room—a cozy space with rustic beams and a primitive hearth used for informal dining.

OPPOSITE: A bay window and sitting space along a hallway allow abundant daylight to pass through the interior windows of an office. ABOVE: We glazed the long corridor leading from the office area to the owners' suite, inserting a furnished niche at the midpoint to create a needed moment of repose.

ABOVE AND OPPOSITE: We saw the stone-clad bedroom, at the terminus of one of the wings, as having originally been a detached utilitarian outbuilding, perhaps a dairy or stable. Within the room, stone walls and rough-hewn beams envelope a quiet seating area wrapped in glass.

OPPOSITE AND FOLLOWING SPREAD: Given the exceptional beauty of the location, multiple outdoor rooms and gardens allow the family to thoroughly enjoy the surrounding splendor and abundant seasonal harvests. ABOVE: The carriage house provides additional guest quarters above and a workshop below, while visually connecting visitors to the main house across the creek via a stone bridge.

LANGUAGE LESSONS
VISION AS OBSERVATION

Being the new kid is never easy. But when my family moved from Buffalo, New York, to southeastern Massachusetts, and I enrolled in the local high school, the transition proved to be difficult in an entirely unexpected way. The first day, I raised my hand, asked if I could visit the bathroom and use the water fountain—and everyone laughed at me! Even the teacher gave me a hard time. *Was I going to take a bath?* No, I needed the restroom. *Was I going to take a rest?* Finally, he got to the point. "You mean you want to use the *lavatory*"—a word with which I was entirely unfamiliar—"and as for the fountain, we call it the *bubbler*"—pronounced "bub-lah," in a fine New England accent that only added to my confusion. Never mind my teenage embarrassment—the cultural dislocation was astonishing. We'd moved a mere 400 miles, and I couldn't understand what anyone was talking about.

What I didn't know then, and have been reminded of repeatedly since, is that there are regions within regions, and it takes time, patience, and sensitivity to discern the subtle differences between them. As my high school experience suggests, it's not unlike learning a foreign language. You can, with study, become fluent in another tongue. But when you try out your knowledge in its country of origin, inevitably you experience startling changes in pronunciation, usage, etiquette, and even slang as you travel from place to place. Architecture is no different. Small variations in location can translate into major alterations in style and form.

One of the first regions into which the firm ventured beyond our southern roots was the small, storied group of eastern Long Island communities known as the Hamptons, where you'll find the three houses that follow. Each in its own way is a "classic" Hamptons house. Architecturally speaking, however, one size most assuredly did not fit all. As we immersed ourselves in the local language, we were required to interpret it in three entirely different ways.

The first instance involved reinventing, for a young family, an 1840s Bridgehampton farmhouse, one that had already endured several less-than-forgiving alterations and additions. In order to coax out the home's full potential, we distilled the narrative into a single story with a clear timeline and—even more critically—extensively transformed the building's relationship to the site without losing the patina and charm of the setting.

The second project proved challenging in an entirely different way. Our clients were stewards of an early twentieth-century seaside "cottage" on the outskirts of East Hampton, and requested that we add new architecture that complemented, but still deferred to, the existing house. The solution, a typical Hamptons "telescope" structure, drew on a local convention that allowed us to modestly meet our clients' hospitality and service needs.

Our third experience grew out of two long-standing Hamptons traditions—pool parties and summer dinner gatherings—filtered through a present-day culture of bed-and-breakfasts, seasonal rentals, and a modern take on the idea of welcoming friends into one's home. The clients sought a hybrid of country house and boutique inn, and looked to these precedents not just for inspiration, but to inform how they and their guests would use the house. It fell to us to stir these historical precedents into a lively new cocktail, one ideal for the making of present-day memories.

Three projects, for three different Hamptons experiences—admittedly, a lot to learn. But taking pains to get each one right—in terms of architecture, lifestyle, and tone—ultimately made us feel that we spoke the language as fluently as the locals.

PAGE 60 AND ABOVE: Toward the end of the design process, detailed illustrations enable us to complete the overarching narrative of a home with our clients. On page 60 are different takes on Long Island vernacular farmhouses; the illustrations above convey nuanced differences between a guest house and carriage house, both on the same property.

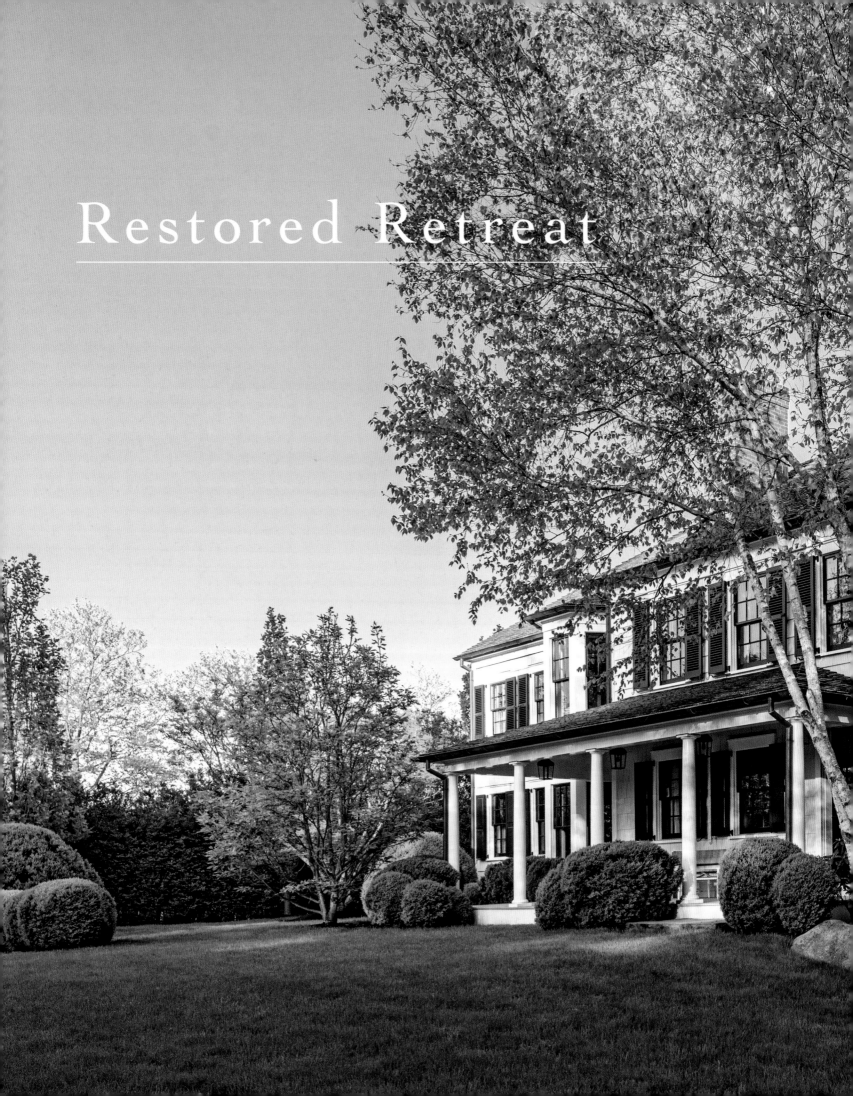

Restored Retreat

PREVIOUS SPREAD, OPPOSITE, AND RIGHT: Our most impactful gesture involved not only the house, but also the front and side yards of this Bridgehampton, Long Island, residence. The entire lawn was regraded, and the land elevated so that the front porch—previously perched awkwardly above the lawn and accessed via a flight of stairs (RIGHT) now sits comfortably at ground level (OPPOSITE).

T his house, in the village of Bridgehampton, occupies a unique position in these pages: it is the only one that wasn't designed and built from scratch. Still, it remains among my very favorite projects, having emerged from imaginative solutions to head-scratching problems—a preexisting historic structure with haphazard additions, on a corner lot with notable disadvantages.

The home, a summer retreat for a family with three children, had been built in stages, the first being a modest farmhouse dating from the 1840s. One wing, thought to be Bridgehampton's Colonial-era schoolhouse, had been appended to the farmhouse shortly after it was completed, with subsequent additions in the 1870s and early 1900s. Each of these components had their charms, and their challenges. Dormers forced into the attic of the schoolhouse had damaged its timber frame, while the other additions were completely out of character, notably

the Italianate tower capped by a "witch's hat" roof, its peculiarity amplified by low-pitched shed structures connecting to the second floor.

But the biggest challenge by far was the site. In front, instead of being nestled into the lawn, the house sat roughly five feet above grade, its porch up a flight of steps as though balanced awkwardly on stilts, and on full display to the public street. Making matters worse, the driveway—entered perilously from the intersection—led to the back of the house, shifting the property's focus to the rear, at the tightest part of the L-shaped lot. As a result, family members forsook their front yard and did their outdoor living in the short, narrow leg of the L. Our immediate goal was to alleviate the cheek-by-jowl experience with their close-at-hand neighbors, and instead take full advantage of the sweeping front yard.

Big challenges demand bold strokes, the first of which addressed the grounds. We shifted the driveway

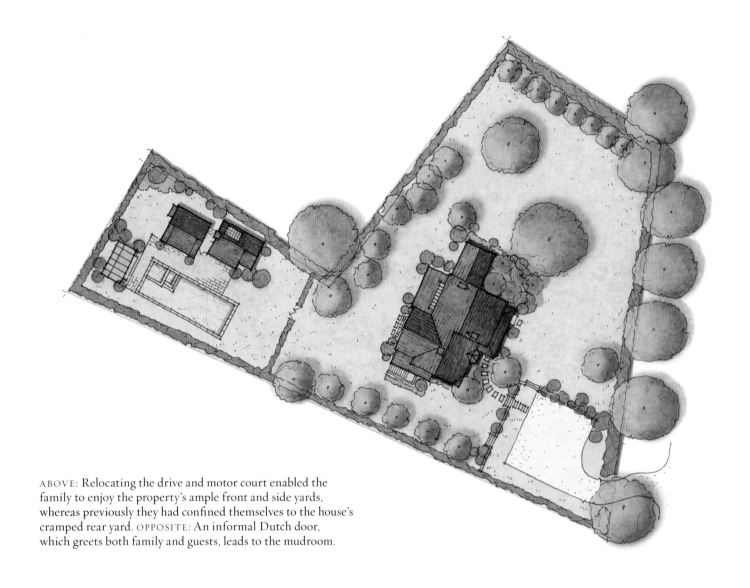

ABOVE: Relocating the drive and motor court enabled the
family to enjoy the property's ample front and side yards,
whereas previously they had confined themselves to the house's
cramped rear yard. OPPOSITE: An informal Dutch door,
which greets both family and guests, leads to the mudroom.

and auto court to the opposite side of the property,
making it at once safer and less conspicuous. The entire
front lawn was then raised up several feet so that the
house floated just above ground level, transforming the
"front-porch-on-stilts" into a relaxed veranda. Finally,
the front and side yards were concealed behind an eight-
foot-deep wall of privet and holly, converting the
formerly exposed property into a private oasis. With a
new parking area tucked discreetly behind boxwoods,
what had once been a dead zone became an active,
welcoming part of the landscape.

The house, too, benefited from transformative
gestures, particularly on the south side. The tower and
shed structures were removed, and the entire rear corner
reconceived. On the ground floor, what had been the
cramped kitchen was enlarged and expanded into a
generously windowed garden-level living room. Above it,
in a new cross gable, we placed a soaring owners' suite,
beside a snug office (overlooking the pool in the backyard)
that doubles as a warm-weather sleeping porch. While we
raised the land in front, we lowered it in back, giving us
much-needed ceiling height in the living room.

In collaboration with interior designer Steven Gambrel, we sifted through the multiple, and at times competing, layers of architecture to find a singular identity for the house, leading us to preserve the front porch, hexagonal two-story bay windows, and the two original staircases. With those elements intact, we worked with Steven to breathe new life into the kitchen, living room, den, and adjoining outdoor living spaces.

As for the former schoolhouse, our intervention was simple yet grand. We scrapped the second floor, and its offending dormers (replacing them with windows more in keeping with the original form), and converted the structure into a light-filled, story-and-a-half space that serves as the den. It's no longer a suitable setting for studying the three R's, but rather a celebration of the simple art of building—and, not least, the fine art of taking it easy.

Ultimately, our subtractions and additions played off of the existing structure in a way that feels both fresh and familiar, historical and timeless. A core value of our firm is stewardship, and this residence afforded opportunities—within and without—to protect, and enhance, history. And to be able to do this for a young family ensures the house will have a future for generations to come.

Behind the glazed internal screen wall at right we set the laundry and powder room. The wall's transparency lets the mudroom receive abundant sunlight, particularly in the afternoon, while the shades and translucent restoration glass provide privacy.

OPPOSITE AND ABOVE: The mudroom door is directly on axis with the new living room at the back of the house. While we raised the landscape in front, we lowered it in the rear to give the living room as much head height as possible. The room's footprint was also enlarged and windows were added on two sides. Despite these alterations, we were able to preserve the quirky charm of the original winding staircase behind the fireplace.

ABOVE: Floor-to-ceiling windows brighten the ground-level living room and reveal the lush landscaping. OPPOSITE: Formerly the living room, the new kitchen has windows creating a ribbon of glass that slides open directly to the skylighted screened porch (perfect for serving summer meals).

PAGES 76 AND 77: Views of the kitchen (with a previously existing fireplace), the pocket bar, and the double-height den (located in a former Colonial-era schoolhouse). OPPOSITE: The combined bedroom and sitting area in the owners' suite overlook the backyard and pool. ABOVE: The adjacent bath with corner views of the front gardens.

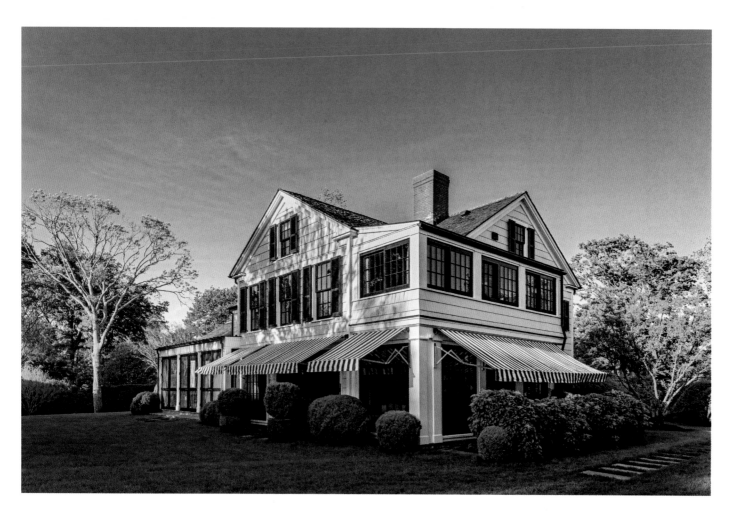

We demolished the entire rear corner of the original house, including its incongruous tower (RIGHT) and reconstructed it (OPPOSITE AND ABOVE), placing the owners' suite upstairs in the cross-gable. The study, sleeping porch, and bath are located in the adjoining glassed-in porch volume.

The original shed structures in the backyard (LEFT) were restyled as a pool house and poolside dining terrace (ABOVE AND OPPOSITE).

Once an underused, unwelcoming afterthought, now the narrow leg of the L-shaped property serves as an enjoyable summertime pool and party area—the perfect retreat for a young, active family.

Seaside Ensemble

Rising above the dunes on the East Hampton seashore is a stately 1916 residence, designed in the Classical Revival style by Grosvenor Atterbury. Upon acquiring the estate and spending a few seasons discovering its splendors, the owners realized that they needed to expand—to provide more space for visiting guests, larger entertaining areas for festive gatherings, and service areas for staff. Instead of adding onto the main house, they chose to preserve its architectural integrity, and acquired a trio of lots positioned just below the house and set back from the shore. Our clients had two clear directives: they did not want a clone of Atterbury's architecture, and the new structures had to be subordinate in scale to the main house. Our response was to create an aesthetically sympathetic ensemble, with a carriage barn at one end, a guesthouse on the opposite side, and between the two, a great lawn enlivened by vegetable and flower gardens and an orchard.

The guesthouse was styled to resemble one of the historic telescope houses that proliferate across Long Island's eastern precincts. Though a relatively straightforward structure, the guesthouse design was in fact driven by an invented narrative we devised, one that both supports the interior program and positions the house comfortably within its surroundings. In our "history," the original two-story component was constructed in 1760; it received a kitchen extension in 1810; and the two telescope pieces enlarged the living quarters in 1840. The project's interior designer, Steven Gambrel, who has worked frequently in the region and possesses a deep knowledge of local building styles, influenced our efforts, helping us to make the completed building more authentic in both plan and detail.

The convention of the telescope house proved equally advantageous in designing the interior. Each volume created subtly defined zones, allowing us to group the six bed-and-bath suites (and a subterranean bunk room) in such a way that the family's guests, who may have only just met, can comfortably coexist under one roof. This artful randomness is enhanced via an unusual circulation pattern: while guests can move up and down freely in the two end wings, they can only go back and forth between them at the basement and second-floor levels. The single way to travel between them on the ground floor is by crossing an open-air dining and living space, in the form of a large covered breezeway, which fosters social interaction while providing buffer areas for privacy.

We continued the architectural progression across the main lawn to the low-slung carriage barn, with its hipped roof, shed dormers, and strap-hinged doors. Avoiding architectural embellishment, the carriage barn draws on the region's more austere Colonial precedents; matching its utilitarian appearance, the structure incorporates parking bays and garden storage at the

PREVIOUS SPREAD: This guesthouse, created for an East Hampton estate, epitomizes the "telescope house"—a vernacular typology that refers to adjoining volumes that descend in size. OPPOSITE: Carefully configured axial views connect the guesthouse to the carriage barn beyond.

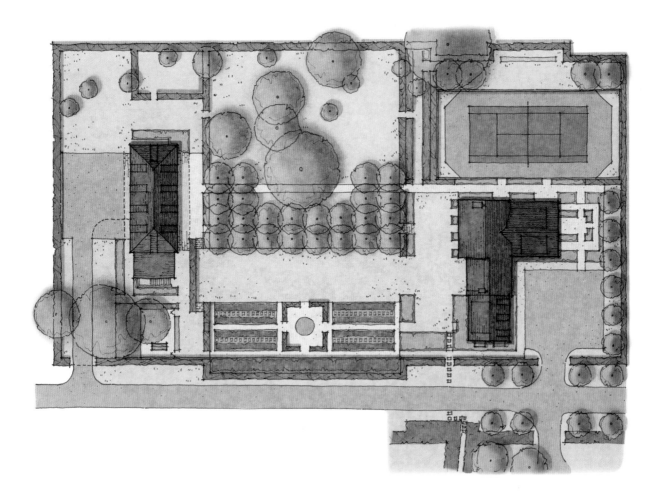

ground level while tucking ship-snug staff quarters above, reminiscent of a nineteenth-century boardinghouse.

Our firm worked closely with the landscape architect Thomas Woltz to nestle the guesthouse and carriage barn within a suite of exterior "rooms," connecting them to one another with views across the property. Leading back to the main house, a pedestrian path follows the natural slope of the terrain and branches off between the hedges to hidden trails, which find their way to out-

door sculptures and activity spaces.

The shared architectural DNA of the buildings, crisp interiors that reflect a familiar palette, and the organized yet relaxed landscape all converge to produce an effect at once timeless and contemporary. We were able to achieve that trickiest, and most satisfying, of outcomes: an estate where architectural tradition and history still reign, while making way for a new generation of buildings.

ABOVE: Our clients acquired a trio of adjoining lots that, working with landscape architect Thomas Woltz, we combined into a single experience: gardens, an orchard, and an expanse of green lawn, enclosed by the carriage barn on one side (seen at left) and the guesthouse on the other. OPPOSITE: A view of the substantial vegetable garden and harvest table with a chicken coop and the carriage house in the background.

PAGES 92 AND 93: The guesthouse's covered breezeway, designed for outdoor living and alfresco dining, affords the only ground-floor connection between the structure's two end wings. ABOVE AND OPPOSITE: The building's exterior modesty gives way, just past the entrance, to a dramatic surprise: a soaring family room, two and a half stories in height, with windows and doors that open directly onto the lawn and the orchard.

ABOVE AND OPPOSITE: In keeping with the idea of a building that expanded sporadically over generations, we created different-sized, informal, interstitial spaces that offer guests the opportunity to be comfortably alone or enjoy one another's company.

OPPOSITE AND ABOVE: The kitchen was designed to facilitate casual self-service by guests, but is easily closed off from the adjoining library (ABOVE), which doubles as an intimate dining room.
PAGES 100 AND 101: Simple materials are detailed in interesting ways throughout the guesthouse.

OPPOSITE: The gravel path leading from the kitchen wing—constructed, in our narrative, perpendicular to the main structure in 1810—leads to the herb garden. ABOVE: The carriage barn, with its flush-mounted lockboxes and strap-hinged barn doors, avoids architectural over-embellishment.

The carriage barn features an open bay with the entrance to the staff quarters on the right and bifold carriage doors to garage bays on the left. The open bay visually connects to the guesthouse in the distance.

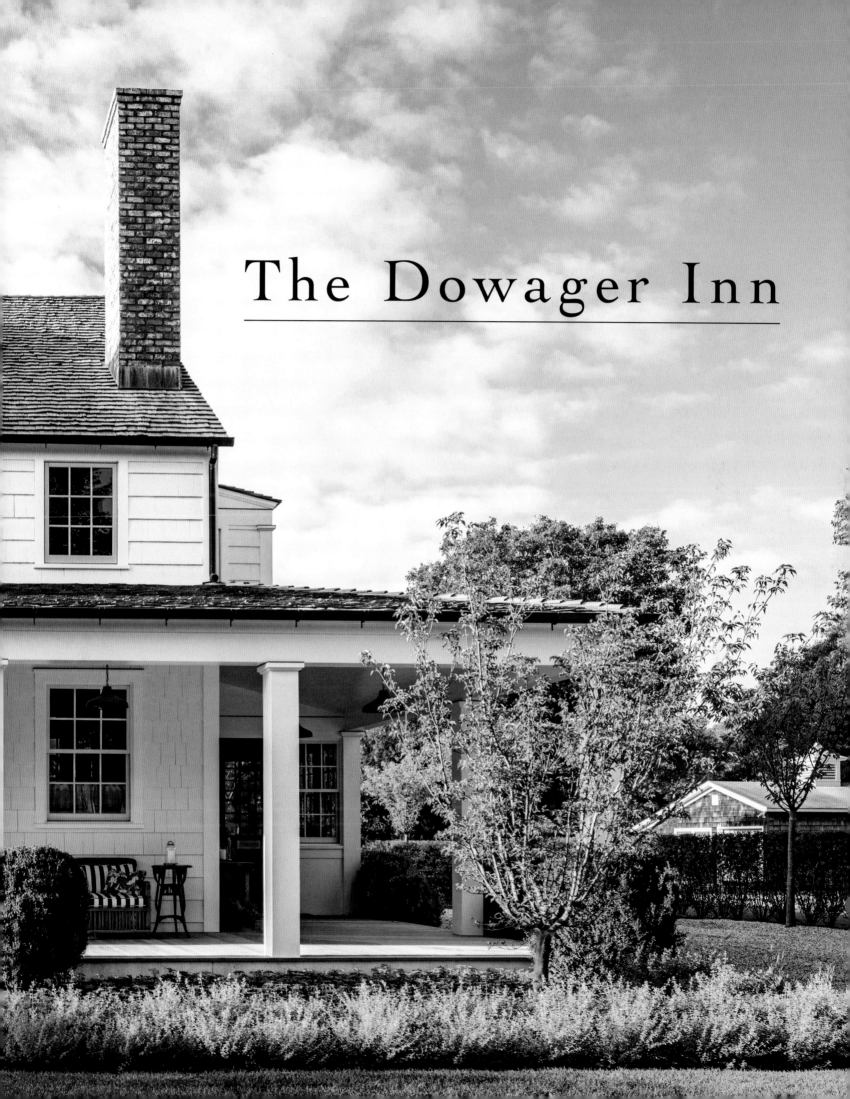

The Dowager Inn

In any architectural project we undertake, the most important considerations are the personality, needs, and dreams of our clients. Though this is always the case, it was perhaps a bit more so with the couple who commissioned this seven-bedroom residence in East Hampton. This was the first home they were creating together—and one of them, an interior designer, had a particularly appealing story he wished to tell. A cheerful Anglophile with a hospitality background, Bryan Graybill's vision was deeply informed by a penchant, shared with his husband, for the clubby and elegant dining rooms, lounges, and bars found in the chic London hotels of Mayfair, Soho, and Marylebone. With a passion for hosting their friends (both local and from "across the pond") from spring through fall, he was clear about not wanting a suburban-style dwelling. He sought instead an *experience*, in which their circle would feel glamorously attended to in both communal and private spaces. It was an interesting challenge, to say the least—and produced a house that combines the flavor of a stylish English hotel with the easy-going pleasures of Hamptons life.

Our clients' international sources of inspiration notwithstanding, we felt it essential to invest the home with a direct connection to local history. Accordingly, we looked to the precedents of eastern Long Island's South Shore to develop an architectural backstory, one that would credibly anchor our clients' playful narrative. The building began its life, in our telling, as a Colonial farmhouse, converted by its eventual owner, an eccentric dowager, in the late 1800s into a village inn and tavern;

in the 1920s, after taking the Grand Tour, our imaginary heroine remodeled the interiors to adopt the Vienna Secessionist and English Arts and Crafts flourishes to which she was exposed in Europe. This useful fiction wasn't a stretch: all of the Hamptons offer delightful examples of farmhouses and village homes that have been transformed into inns as distinctive as the setting envisioned by our clients. Armed with this timeline—and its accompanying colorful narrative—we could proceed with both program and precedent firmly in place.

The communal spaces derive their kick from the twinning of surprise and delight. Instead of a conventional vestibule, the entry serves as a stylistic take on an inglenook that is part banquette, part pew, with an understated fireplace at its center—a cozy space that creates an instant sense of arrival and anticipation. From here you enter the grand salon and experience the home's full amplitude via a wall of glass overlooking the pool and gardens. As if the view were not intoxicating enough, the salon offers the assurance of a good time with a freestanding, fully equipped mahogany bar.

A stroll past the bar leads to the open kitchen and "orangerie," English country-inspired spaces with chalk-white, textured brick walls and appealingly sturdy furnishings in lieu of built-in cabinetry. But it's the intuitive plan that creates the charm. Guests and residents alike understand where to sit and stand, where to find the coffee and tea, the cutting boards and knives—a relaxed and enjoyable shared experience that's been carefully designed yet feels entirely natural.

PREVIOUS SPREAD: In the invented history of this East Hampton residence, the farmhouse volume with the covered porch sheltering the front door was built first in the mid-1700s, with the adjoining gabled element added in the late 1800s.
OPPOSITE: The house is separated from the street by a front garden and privet hedge, with the side porch facing the motor court.

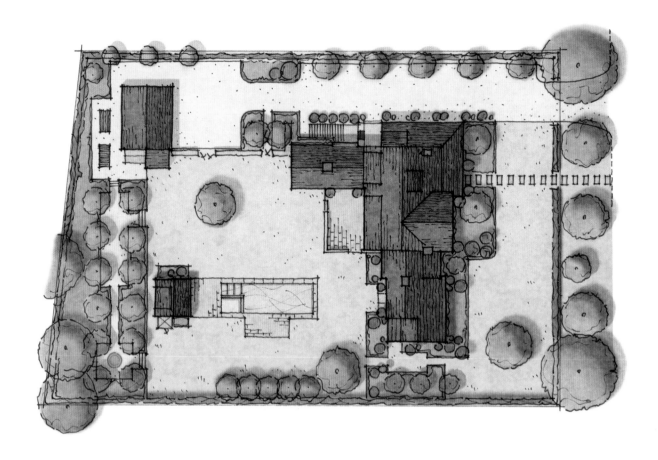

Guest suites received the same sort of small, impactful gestures characteristic of a thoughtful host. Both the upstairs and downstairs vestibules offer quiet moments of repose for guests to share. At the upper landing, a skylighted library serves as an antechamber serving four suites. On the lower level, two bedrooms share a tavern-inspired breakfast nook (or tasting room, depending on the time of day) that encourages easy sociability. And while they share a cohesive design palette, each of the suites has been individualized, capturing the particularity and flair of a small London hotel, and evoking a sense of familiarity for visitors often far from home.

By embracing a diversity of inspirations, we created a canvas sufficiently welcoming and flexible to accept and absorb our clients' often exotic interests and selections. Our references, actual and fictional (from both sides of the Atlantic), encouraged a joyful embrace of quirk and imperfection. These helped us to conjure a sure sense of authenticity, one that reminds both residents and guests to relax, stay awhile, and not take matters too seriously—emotions essential to the spirit of a house that is, above all, a gift to one's friends.

ABOVE: The house was specifically sited to engage with a series of ancillary buildings and outdoor "rooms."
OPPOSITE: At the rear of the property, behind the pool and pool house, we animated what otherwise would have been an unused landscape buffer with a raised, tree-lined sitting area and alfresco dining space, defined by pea gravel, boxwoods, and granite steps.

ABOVE: We sought to make the most of the backyard by providing a variety of ways to enjoy it. The covered porch incorporates a fireplace for the shoulder seasons and sometimes cool summer evenings. RIGHT: In a nod to the region's Colonial-era building practices, the pool house features asymmetrical, paneled doors and random-width siding.

ABOVE AND RIGHT: Styled to resemble an inglenook, the entry features a whimsical portrait by artist George Condo that establishes the spirit of the home. A discreet hallway, with mahogany planking and thoughtfully placed brass coat hooks, connects the entry to the grand salon.

ABOVE AND OPPOSITE: The grand salon, which looks out onto both the front and rear yards, proclaims the structure's dual identity as home and hostelry with a fully equipped, freestanding mahogany bar. High-gloss lacquer finishes on the millwork and ceiling add a touch of glamour, influenced by the Vienna Secession movement.

Multiple seating areas present a range of experiential opportunities and enable the grand salon to be comfortably enjoyed by gatherings both large and intimate. The front windows, with their tactile brass hardware, open the room completely to the front garden and street beyond, welcoming guests "home."

The English Arts and Crafts and Vienna Secession influences are evident in the decorative motifs and furnishings, and also resonate deeply in the interior architectural details of the doors, windows, panels, and wainscoting found throughout the house.

ABOVE: Off of the kitchen is the larder, a true "workhorse" room serving as a pantry, catering kitchen, coffee bar, and informal entry. RIGHT: The chalky brick, wide-plank floors, and overscaled copper lights set the tone for the main kitchen.

Adjacent to the kitchen is a casual dining space dubbed the orangerie, owing to its greenhouse-like character. The open floor space in a traditional orangerie accommodates potted citrus plants—like orange, lemon, and lime trees—that need to winter indoors. In this context, the open space provides circulation for brunch, luncheons, and cocktail parties. The sun-washed banquette next to the fireplace makes the room a pleasure to inhabit in all seasons.

ABOVE AND OPPOSITE: The parlor is an intricately detailed space that serves as a private sitting room leading to the owners' suite but can also comfortably extend the party from the adjacent grand salon.

ABOVE: The shapes and profiles of the millwork in the dressing room reflect the influences of the Vienna Secession and animate the surfaces, eliminating the need for complicated paint treatments. OPPOSITE: The prismatic wainscot paneling and hand-finished plaster walls, which both absorb and reflect light, make the scale of the bedroom feel cozy and well-proportioned, while the vaulted plank ceiling and silk chandelier keep the room light and airy.

PAGE 130: The second-floor stair landing, with its intriguing take on a skylighted library and reading room, offers house guests an unexpected moment of repose. PAGE 131: On the lower level, the red-lacquered screen wall gives distinction and character to a quotidian kitchenette that also serves as a vestibule and gathering space for the guest bedrooms on either side. ABOVE AND OPPOSITE: Working from a cohesive palette, each guest suite retains its own charm and character through a variety of distinct architectural elements. FOLLOWING SPREAD: The pool centers on the owners' suite and sleeping porch.

STYLE
AND INVENTION
VISION AS INTERPRETATION

I've talked about the importance of being sufficiently well versed in a local design language in order to speak it like a native. That invests a house with authenticity, of course, but there's another benefit to this immersion: once you've fully acquainted yourself with the nuances of a style, you can start to experiment with it. A firm grounding in, and sure grasp of, precedent liberates an architect's imagination to transform the status quo in lively ways that nonetheless preserve its integrity and principles. Put another way, we can't break the mold unless we know how the mold got made in the first place.

Consider an example from another medium, the painter Claude Monet. As a young architecture student, I found myself at Boston's Museum of Fine Arts utterly spellbound by the light and atmosphere in his *Rouen Cathedral* series. Seeing those canvases together marked the first time I'd experienced architecture not as something physical or structural, but rather as pure emotion. Whereas some artists create compositions that are vaguely suggestive—inspiring you to speculate on the individuals, actions, and circumstances they portray—none of that is necessary to enjoy a Monet. To understand how you're supposed to feel about one of his paintings, all you have to do is look at it.

Experiencing the pleasures Monet serves up so sublimely, I was reminded that transforming a familiar genre into something that's groundbreaking and original requires a thorough command of tradition. It is the continuum of tradition, serving as backdrop and context, that gives invention its full meaning. Without Vermeer, Rembrandt, and Rubens, Monet's achievements cannot be fully understood or appreciated. The same principle applies to architecture.

Let me quickly add that, in our office, bending the rules is never about novelty. If we challenge architectural precedent, it's to resolve problems; to introduce wit and whimsy; to create homes that clearly "belong," yet extend the possibilities of what belonging might mean; to express more clearly the timeless ideals and traditions that we value so strongly. Most of all, we experiment so that our clients can think freely, and not limit their aspirations to what has already been done.

The three residences on the pages to come are clear examples of this balance between past and present, tradition and invention. Yet as reinterpretations of historical styles, these homes also share some definitive traits, notably a close attention to the needs of our clients and a finely tuned response to their natural settings. The first project transforms Lowcountry craft and building traditions with a crisp approach to detail, one that owes as much to graphic design as to the carpenter's bench. The second house, located on a South Carolina barrier island, reinterprets the classic Charleston single house and its characteristic side-facing piazzas for practical reasons as well as to achieve a signature aesthetic. And for the third, a Long Island estate, we considered the Colonial, Federal, and Shingle Style traditions that dominate in the area, took a step back, and asked, what if all those eighteenth- and nineteenth-century architects had gone in a different direction?

Engaging with a diversity of regions and their corresponding architectures, we use what we learn to unlock our imaginations. And while this continues to make us better architects, I believe it's improved our collaborative skills as well, enabling us to go in multiple creative directions with our clients. Historical Concepts has, to be sure, become associated with a certain kind of design work. But our focus has been less on a signature style and more on a signature method of practice: a way of design that can be applied to any genre of architecture, almost anywhere in the world. To be quite candid, the first aesthetic arrow we release doesn't always hit the mark. But by embracing a design approach that is unafraid of trial and error—one based as much on hard work and dedication as research and invention—we remain open to the alchemy that can turn our clients' aspirations into architectural gold.

We try always to remember that *creative process* is made up of two words, and the emphasis remains firmly on the latter. There are times when we're not completely sure where it will take us. But with the patience and engagement of our patrons, in the end, we get where we need to go—and enjoy the journey of invention every step of the way.

PAGE 136 AND ABOVE: Throughout the design process, we often discover opportunities that require additional exploration. Sketched vignettes, details, and interior perspectives enable us to quickly confirm these new directions with our clients.

The Simple Life

This house, nestled amid the pines and palmettos along a slow-moving stretch of South Carolina's May River, isn't tied to a specific narrative. Neither does it draw excessively on a regional vernacular or classical genre. Rather, it is clean-lined and contemporary: a response to the location, to the spectacular sunlight and unspoiled views, and above all to the owners' desire for a certain kind of life. If there's a historical reference, it is the land, and the simple, relaxed state of being that pervades the Lowcountry.

An architecturally modest residence seemed almost obligatory, given our clients' exceptional site. With abundant oyster beds lining the riverbank, mere yards from the property, there are no docks to disrupt the pristine condition. The view is richly layered, with an ever-changing foreground of grasses and tidal flats, clusters of vegetation, and a green line of forest visible on the far shore. But it's the light that is the truly magical component. The transit of the sun, no matter the season, bestows a sublime array of moods and experiences from early morning to the day's last glow.

Accordingly, the couple requested that all of the rooms, from the airy entertaining spaces to the cozy bedroom quarters, have views of the natural wonders beyond. What's more, the clients were very clear on exactly which views they wanted and why, a process of curation similar to the selection of the artworks found throughout the home. To achieve their objective, we needed to unbundle the house: that is, break down the traditional Lowcountry five-bay, center hall structure and distribute the rooms throughout a series of smaller volumes. Each of these was then tucked unobtrusively into the site, forming its own connections to landscape architect Don Hooten's elegantly designed surroundings.

The plan unfolds across four modest pavilions, each revealing traditional forms and materials but distilled in a way that feels almost contemporary, and connected by hyphens—hallways that use floor-to-ceiling windows to create a fluid connection between the pavilions. At one end lies a generous owners' suite, given privacy from the rest of the house by a shared office on one side, and a master hallway on the other. Then come the major public spaces, the living room pavilion on the left and the open kitchen pavilion to the right, communicating with each other across the skylighted center entry hall. On the house's other side, past the dining room, butler's pantry, and stair hall, lies a pair of guest bedroom suites. The linear plan makes the house easy to understand, and facilitates rooms with natural light and views on two, and often three, sides. The porches and terraces, arranged around the perimeter, capture different exposures and help to blur the line between structure and nature.

Though it wasn't our emphasis, the house's architectural simplicity, enhanced by Havilande Whitcomb's interior design work, can be interpreted as either austere traditionalism or regional modernism. The four cross gables, finished in plain brick and board-and-batten siding, suggest a contemporized version of a nineteenth-century English manor house. For the

PREVIOUS SPREAD: Broken down into a series of relatively modest pavilions that nestle discreetly into the site, this South Carolina house defers to—and becomes one with—the natural beauty of the landscape. OPPOSITE: The view from the back porch.

PREVIOUS SPREAD AND RIGHT:
Don Hooten's landscaped entrance
experience features grasses that
replicate the Lowcountry's
naturally occurring foliage while
crepe myrtles and boxwoods define
the space with a touch of formality.
Brick, board-and-batten, and
standing-seam metal roofs draw
on the regional vernacular
architecture, while large windows
at the entry and connectors give the
house a modern transparency.

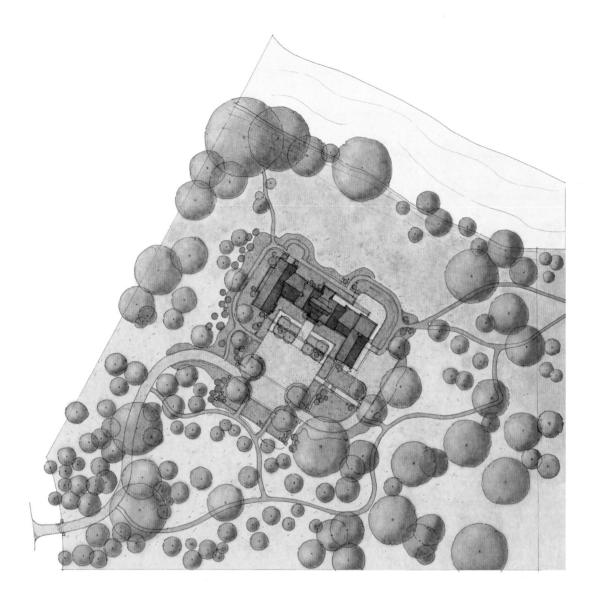

interior, rather than heavy traditional detailing, we took a strongly graphic "cutout" approach, which restates local patterns in a simplified language. Stylized stair rails, newel posts, and balusters—all crisp and angular—create expressionistic effects. Regularly spaced gaps between horizontal wall boards suggest an inverse rendering of the shadows cast by the exterior clapboard. These unexpected touches, inside and out, lightly convey a sense of place while adding a playful overlay to the architecture, one that suits the house and its setting.

As Miles Davis famously observed, "It's not the notes you play, it's the notes you don't play." The same is true for the creation of architecture: knowing when to embellish and when to show restraint. This delicate balancing act captured the spirit of the home, one that is both rooted in place, but also as unique as the landscape that envelops it. The result is a simplicity immediately understood and felt; the perfect home for life in the Lowcountry.

ABOVE: The site plan reveals the design's light-handed approach to the wooded site and broad orientation to the river. OPPOSITE: Directly across from the steel-framed glass front door, on the other side of the entry hall, is an identical wall of glass that opens onto the back terrace and river view.

Crisp lines, clean forms, a custom black marble fireplace, and a striking modern landscape painting anchor the living room. The hallway at left leads to the owners' suite; the opening to the right of the fireplace connects to the library bar and office space beyond.

ABOVE: Beyond the kitchen, the hallway to the guest wing includes a pantry with a stylish porthole window and built-in cabinetry that can also open up to the hall a full-service bar. OPPOSITE: Like the living room, the kitchen, with its twin islands and abundant counter space, enjoys a peaked ceiling and windows on the front and rear facades. FOLLOWING SPREAD: The kitchen as seen from the center entry hall; the dining room at left opens onto the screened porch to fully capture the breezes and views.

ABOVE: In the guest wing, the newel posts, balusters, and articulated wallboards restate the traditions of Lowcountry carpentry in a crisp, bold language reminiscent of modern graphic design. OPPOSITE: The striking lines of the wallboards also cleverly conceal ample closets, allowing the base of the stairs to effectively serve as a boot room.

OPPOSITE AND ABOVE: The soft color palette and subtle detailing of the owners' suite embrace the natural setting by celebrating a comfortable and quiet elegance.

The house's rear elevation reveals the architecture's interplay of open and enclosed spaces, as well as its unity with the landscape. Soft plantings and simple hardscape elements flow seamlessly into the pristine understory and river's edge.

Precedent Redefined

This family compound, on an island off South Carolina's coast, presented us with three challenges that became the keys to what is perhaps the firm's most stylistically inventive architecture to date. Two of them had to do with view management— in effect, flip sides of the same coin. Heads: What's the best response to a stunning panorama? Do you give it all away at once, or allow the experience to unfold gradually? On this island, the issue becomes especially germane, as it's a vivid example of visual revelation. The road winds through an enveloping atmosphere of live oaks, pines, and palmettos, and arrives at an unobstructed vista of grassy wetlands, extending to infinity in all directions. And then there's tails: the close proximity of neighbors. The condition is acute for this popular second-home destination, where properties are small, irregular, and often in one another's views. Under such circumstances, making a house feel like it's alone in nature can require considerable sleight of hand.

But it was the third challenge— keeping pace with an engaged, highly imaginative client—that presented the greatest opportunity. Though she had specific requirements, what she conveyed to us, in a rich narrative that held us all spellbound, was not only architectural but experiential. She wanted big gates, with boldly expressed rivets and stout hinges, opening onto a world within a world. She envisioned an entertainment zone that was part of the immediate landscape. She imagined a grand stair in the living room, with a bar tucked beneath it, floating against a two-story window. She pictured a guest cottage topped by a glass-enclosed writing room. Our client was also focused on how her family and friends would use the house (alone or in small, medium, and large groups) throughout the interior, on the terraces, and around the property.

The sheer number of ideas with which we were presented was, in our experience, nearly unprecedented. So, too, was the task: to take this cornucopia of inspiration and transform it into a work of architecture, at once multifaceted and cohesive.

We began by pondering precedent. This had less to do with style than organization. What kind of house, we asked ourselves, might offer a framework strong yet flexible enough to support our client's vision, and also answer the challenges of context? What made sense for two structures that would be each other's close-at-hand neighbors, in a tidal environment in which the water could, in the course of a day, rise and fall six or eight feet?

Our thinking led to a form that could be naturally adapted for our purposes: the Charleston single house. With its side-yard-facing, sun-shielding piazzas, this precedent was an ideal framework for our client's vision. In particular, the examples found in the city's Battery district, with their upraised floor plates, offered a 200-year-old template that lent itself to contemporary reinterpretation. Making the main house and the guesthouse next-door neighbors mirrored the cozy conditions of Charleston's quaint residential streets, where piazzas look out across gardens and terraces to their neighbors' homes. Most usefully, the piazza precedent could be reinterpreted as glass-enclosed porches that captured the island's vistas—a familiar form, rendered in a contemporary manner.

By making the gates the de facto front door to the residence, the plan creates a threshold that lets the

PREVIOUS SPREAD: The hypnotic view from the house, of shimmering tributaries and grassy marshes, on one of South Carolina's most picturesque coastal islands. OPPOSITE: The architecture draws on the traditions of the historic Charleston single house—in this case, glass-enclosed versions of the stacked piazzas (traditional side-facing porches)—to take full advantage of the panoramic vistas.

residents leave the public world behind and enter one that's entirely their own. Continuing this idea, we worked with the landscape architect Laurie Durden to create outdoor spaces that serve functions usually found within the home—notably the laneway between the two buildings that effectively became the vestibule for both. This garden-level entry gives the project an unusual distinction by launching the residential experience of the home well before you reach the front door.

Two of our client's most effective ideas had little to do with precedent or style, focusing instead on experience. Both appear in the guesthouse. At the very top, we responded to the images of glass-box architecture that she shared by creating a pristine writing studio awash in natural illumination and embracing 270-degree views. At the very bottom, the lap pool flows into a grotto directly beneath the structure—adorned with niches for candlelit lanterns, and with shards of mirrored glass embedded in the ceiling, which by night reflect "starlight" on the water's surface. Neither the minimalist studio nor the romantic cove is what classical architects are typically called upon to do. But as we discovered on this journey, a process with integrity can roam far afield of precedent yet remain consistent with values associated with tradition.

Indeed, if the historic Charleston single house served as our template, it is no less true that, almost immediately, we began reinterpreting and adapting it.

Our client envisioned a dramatic front gate opening onto a subtly landscaped, outdoor "entry hall" between the guesthouse (at left) and the main residence (at right).

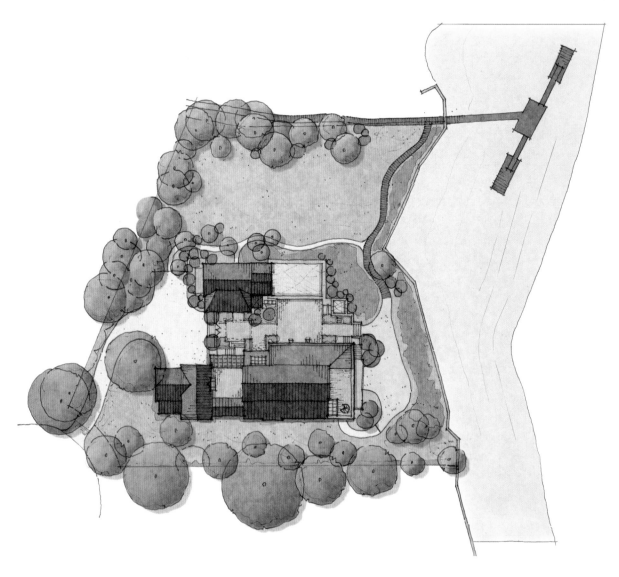

The interior designer Amanda Nisbet collaborated on colorful schemes that remind one that even "serious" architecture can, and should, be fun. As our client remained invested in every space, the process was enjoyably iterative, testing her many ideas within the context of both the precedent and the evolving design. We began by sketching traditional motifs like cornices and pilasters in their classically correct proportions. But often, as the design progressed, these elements became more distilled, or disappeared entirely, existing as classical ghosts behind a contemporary shell, with only their proportions remaining.

These acts of removal, let me add, weren't frivolous. They arose from the principles that give rigor to all our work, classical or otherwise—foremost among them the desire to make our client's dreams come true. In the end, being pushed in new directions was deeply gratifying, and gave us the realization that we can respond to any and all circumstances—while remaining faithful to our cherished classical roots.

ABOVE: The site plan reveals the orientation of the guesthouse and main house to the marsh, and the use of the single-house typology to maximize river views. OPPOSITE: Because the main floor is raised to protect it from tidal surges, an elevated courtyard garden was placed just off to the side of the front door, providing a respite for visitors at the top of the entry stairs.

To sustain the connection to the site and bring light into the core of the house, the communal spaces were arranged with overlapping views that flow seamlessly into one another. Here, the glass wall defining the living room opens onto the elevated courtyard garden, and the interior windows to the left and right of the fireplace share light with the entry hall.

PAGES 172 AND 173: The open kitchen and dining room connect visually but remain defined as separate spaces as a result of changes in ceiling material and color palette. ABOVE AND OPPOSITE: Our client envisioned a copper-clad bar, tucked beneath a grand stair set against an expansive window, a tantalizing architectural element enhanced by exquisite, hand-forged metalwork at the stair rail.

174

OPPOSITE: The owners' suite features a private river-facing veranda, with a floor-to-ceiling wall of glass that draws light into the bath and reflects views of the water. ABOVE: This intimate corner in the bedroom offers breathtaking views at all times of day.

ABOVE: The corridor connecting the living room to the children's wing—glazed on both sides for a treehouse-like effect—also features a discreet shelf for setting down drinks, should the party spill over from the living room. OPPOSITE: The bunk room offers a playful surprise with its expressive use of materials and detailing.

178

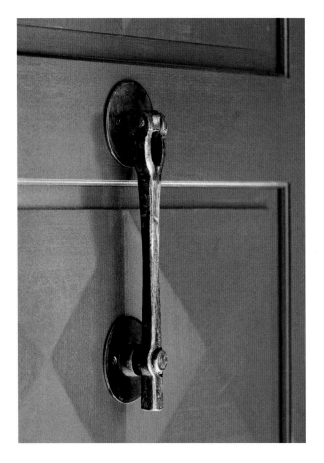

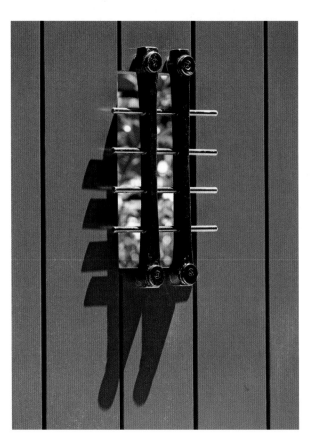

PAGES 180 AND 181: Bold iron hardware elements, found on both the interior and exterior, create a cohesive palette and infuse the architecture with an overlay of handcraftsmanship. ABOVE: The entrance to the guesthouse has an almost urban quality, evoking the spirit of historic Charleston. OPPOSITE: A waterside veranda is one of the multiple opportunities to enjoy the natural wonders of the property and the marsh.

ABOVE: The conservatory-like writing studio atop the guesthouse answered our client's desire for a "glass box" in which to work. OPPOSITE: A layered view from the sleeping porch of the main house, looking toward the guesthouse, pool patio, and horizon.

OPPOSITE AND ABOVE: Bridging the natural and the man-made, the lap pool slips beneath
the guesthouse into an architectural grotto. Our client requested that bits of mirrored glass be
embedded in the ceiling to reflect candlelight as a continuation of the stars in the night sky.

The density of the project, borrowed from Charleston's historic Battery district, comfortably fits a complicated architectural program into a constrained site—creating outdoor rooms and framed views that enhance the connection to the majesty of the South Carolina coast.

It Takes a Village

"I want a village," our client said.

It was our first conversation. And as he explained what he had in mind for an expansive site beside the wetlands edging one of Long Island's storied bays, it emerged that the house was going to be quite large, and with multiple requirements. Yet by invoking the village model, our client expressed a novel, and most appealing, idea. He proposed that we break up and distribute the home's program across the site, interweaving it with outdoor rooms and gardens, to create a rich variety of human-scaled experiences. Anyone who's ever explored a picturesque New England village knows the pleasures of discovery it brings. Our challenge was to replicate that village sensibility, but in a single residence, thereby affording multiple ways to enjoy both the house and its surroundings.

In concert with the interior designer Steven Gambrel and landscape designer Tom Janczur, we organized the property into three distinct zones, each with its own character. The sweeping entry drive, flanked by a lush lawn and walled garden, establishes the mood. This is followed by a motor court—framed by a bicycle barn, carriage house, and breezeway—that introduces the house and sets the stage for the entry. Beyond the residence, a rambling meadow and floral landscape flow down to the wetlands and the bay beyond—a precinct, bookended by the pool house and artist's studio, that's perfect for savoring all the summer season has to offer.

Just as we wanted to avoid the beach house cliché, we also hoped to depart from the prevailing local style. Across eastern Long Island, there is a legacy of Colonial,

Federal, and Georgian residential architecture, as well as the ubiquitous Shingle Style, and it occurred to us that our atypical approach offered the opportunity to shake up the narrative. While the English Colonial influence is evident throughout the region, there were also Dutch and Belgian precedents. So we thought it would be fun to ask, what if one of *those* traditions had been dominant? Though each was distinct, there were moments where the styles crossed paths, and we sought to find a synthesis between them: to create something original and new, yet familiar and rooted in place.

As with many of our projects, we created a narrative to suggest how the "village" might have evolved over time. While sometimes this is expressed via a mix of complementary and contrasting architectural volumes, we told this particular story with our choices of material and exterior finishes. On the front and rear facades, we interspersed oak posts, beams, lintels, and corbels among lime-washed brick walls and gables to suggest infill elements, enclosures, and additions. We also left the oak unfinished, with the weathering patterns telling a story of rain and wind, sun and shadow, across the seasons.

Inside, our multilayered narrative drew inspiration from the canvases of Johannes Vermeer. In his work, the Dutch master's exquisite use of softly glowing sunlight to suggest a quiet intimacy is enhanced by architectural backdrops that balance airiness and containment. Accordingly, we made extensive use of large casement windows, operable interior transoms, Dutch doors, and glass screen walls—all devices that define spaces without absolutely enclosing them. To this mix were added robust

PREVIOUS SPREAD AND OPPOSITE: Flanked by walled gardens and outbuildings, a broad graveled motor court at the end of the driveway serves as an outdoor vestibule—the formal moment of welcome to this Long Island house.

The front facade, which combines Dutch and Belgian influences, tells the story of a house that evolved over time. Oak elements (left unfinished to record the patina from the region's dramatic weather patterns), inserted between the lime-washed brick gables, suggest enclosures and additions.

Off the motor court, a rustic porte cochere affords covered access to the family entrance and mudroom (to the right) and a carriage barn with a caretaker's apartment above (to the left). The post-and-beam motif, paired with concrete pedestals, draws on an early agrarian form. Together with the guest wing (on the far side of the motor court), the structure frames the arrival experience.

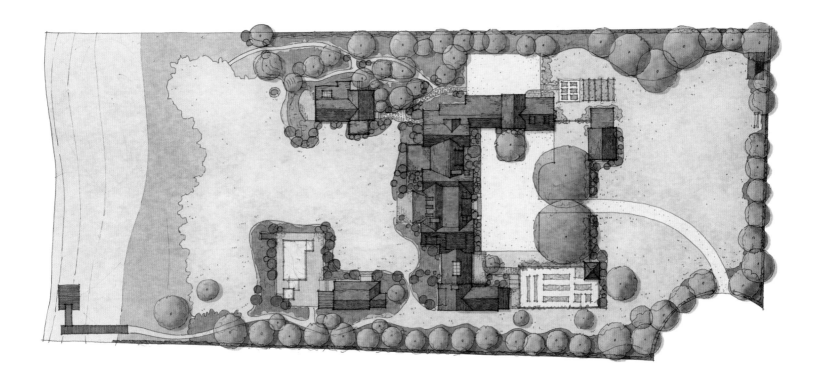

ceiling beams and dark mullions, as well as light-absorptive plaster and reflective paint. In combination with the semitransparent spaces, these materials convey solidity and porosity, an air of contemplation and an embrace of the outdoors—a mood at once highly atmospheric and satisfyingly casual.

Upstairs, the tone is lighter, the plan more loosely defined. Rather than creating a private master sitting room with water views, our clients requested a family-friendly gathering area just outside the owners' suite, overlooking the front courtyard and garden. The other upstairs spaces are arranged along an enfilade, yet changes in width, scale, material, and light produce an experiential richness that keeps it from feeling like a hallway, providing a different sense of arrival for each bedroom suite.

A similar sensibility comes into play beyond the residence. The outbuildings are arranged across from one another, each visually connecting with the main house, while the outdoor rooms in between them layer, direct, and elongate the views across the property to the water. Lounging and dining areas, covered and exposed, firepits and sun terraces, pool decks and gardens, woodland trails and mown meadow paths all afford multiple ways to enjoy the natural setting of this singular "village."

Creating a narrative of "what could have been" sparked our imaginations and led to surprisingly inventive results. The outcome is a home with the spirit of a village that's both welcoming and inspiring, whimsical and serious—not what you were expecting, but entirely appropriate and comfortable nonetheless.

OPPOSITE: At the side entry to the studio, Tom Janczur's landscaping suggests the lush prosaic character of a European woodland garden. ABOVE: The site plan reveals four distinct outdoor experiences: the forelawn and entry drive; the walled vegetable garden and motor court; the expansive back lawn and gardens; and the pristine wetland meadow edging the bay.

The entry offers the first of the home's many layers of discovery: rather than a modestly scaled foyer or vestibule, one enters into a grand hall with a boldly patterned tile floor, muscular beams, and woodwork lacquered in black. Light from the broad glass Dutch door and sidelights plays off the warm plaster walls.

ABOVE AND OPPOSITE: The grand entry has the robust character of a banquet hall, with its long formal dining table, substantial hearth, and comfortable inglenook overlooking the motor court. The interior glass doors and operable transoms, and the interplay of sun and shadow that they create, harken back to the genre scenes of the Dutch masters.

PAGE 204: The light-washed stair hall features a bay window overlooking the walled garden. PAGE 205: The capacious mudroom, accessed from the porte cochere, features cubbies for organizing the family's gear, a substantial package table, and a custom concrete basin for washing dogs. ABOVE AND OPPOSITE: Richly figured stone and colorful accents animate the kitchen. The warm gray palette, chamfered beams, and well-proportioned windows soften the scale of an otherwise bold domestic space.

PAGES 208 AND 209: An intricate plaster ceiling and expressive, linear millwork are highlighted by a varied paint scheme, which creates a continuous framework for books, artwork, and views in this bay-facing library. RIGHT: The upstairs family sitting room (just outside the owners' suite) is tucked into the eaves with large casement windows opening onto the walled gardens below.

ABOVE AND OPPOSITE: The owners' bedroom, with its lofty ceiling and dormer windows, effortlessly incorporates a pair of club chairs, a settee, and a sofa in a cozy lounge arrangement. The room also enjoys a private covered porch overlooking the back lawn and gardens, with views of the bay in the distance.

On the water-facing side of the house, floor-to-ceiling divided-light windows draw from the home's Dutch and Belgian influences while providing a more modern spirit. The extensive glazing also dematerializes the separation between the interior living room and the exterior sun terrace.

OPPOSITE AND ABOVE: The house's gently downsloping back lawn is the setting for several outbuildings, including this combination workshop and artist studio, which looks toward the pool house. FOLLOWING SPREAD: Tucked between the guest wing and pool (with its whimsical "dock to nowhere" at the edge of the seagrass meadow), a freestanding pavilion serves as the pool house and gym.

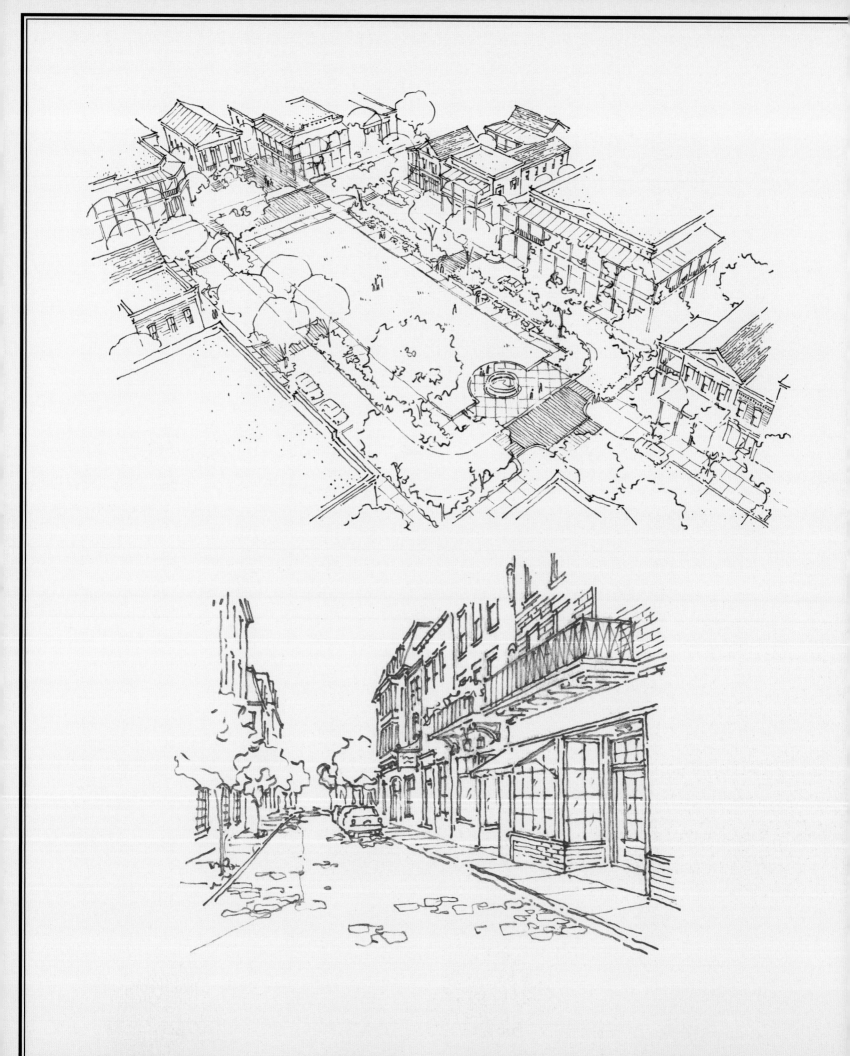

THE HOME BEYOND
VISION AS LEGACY

There is a special satisfaction to be had from helping an individual or family turn a residential dream into reality, a pleasure that I hope is evident on every page of this book. Yet over time, our long-term engagement with the idea of home has led us to consider its larger implications: specifically, how the manifestations of private life, its special joys and consolations, can be extended into the public realm. How the idea of home connects to the idea of community, I believe, lies in what might be described as Historical Concepts' foundation story—a vision that Jim Strickland has, at one time or another, shared with us all.

As he relates in the introduction to this book, Jim grew up in Buckhead among many of Atlanta's great architectural treasures. But he didn't come from a wealthy family. "My folks lacked the means to create their dream home," he recalls, "and I believed that if I combined my love of Southern residential classicism with the building and development knowledge I'd amassed through my career, I could design houses that the average working man or woman—people like my parents—could enjoy. I wanted to create homes about which they could say, when they walked in every night after work, 'Wow—I can't believe I'm living like this.'"

Jim recognized that not everyone has the wherewithal to commission a custom-designed residence. But the core of his ambition—that everyone, no matter their circumstances, should be able to wonder at the beauty in their lives—has affected all of us in a deep and profound way, and directly influenced our work. Designing the kinds of buildings that give shape and sustenance to our communities stands as our next frontier.

It begins with the simplest of questions: What is home? Or, more specifically, what becomes "home" when we walk out our own front door? It's the places where we work, we worship, we celebrate, where we relax and recharge. Going from home to hometown, we seek out places that nurture and inspire us, encourage and support us—and their design involves many of the same considerations as crafting small residences or family estates. Precedent and style, region and site, collaboration and imagination all impact town planning and, in particular, public buildings (whether cultural, institutional, commercial, or recreational). The intimate narrative of a well-designed public space—that inviting bench on a tree-lined street, the bustling farmer's market in the plaza, a bandstand in the meadow of a park—speaks to many of the same longings for connection and belonging that we find in our personal homes.

In fact, the project that follows, Ashbourne Farms, actually began life as a family farm in rural Kentucky. As such, it was layered with generations of hard work, thoughtful expansion and, of course, cherished memories. To successfully transform the original "show barn" into an event space and concert hall—a place where friends and visitors could make memories of their own by celebrating life's shared milestones—demanded sensitivity to precedent, context, and reinterpretation all at once. Our client proceeded from the conviction that, sometimes, the only way to sustain a home is by opening it up to others. There was much that needed to be accomplished, but the most important task (the one we held in our hearts and heads throughout) was to provide a setting in which new memories could be made without banishing the old ones.

For these reasons, I thought it most fitting that Ashbourne Farms should conclude this story. By taking Jim's original philosophy of "drawing from the past to design the architecture of today—and tomorrow" and applying it to the world beyond the home, we're able to extend what we offer to one and all. As Historical Concepts continues to expand and evolve, I look forward to seeing where this will lead us.

But this I know: wherever we go, the journey will be personal. We are as captivated by the simple country dwellings and quirky outbuildings that enrich the rural landscape as by the stately homes and grand estates that grace the pages of this book. And we are equally intrigued by the restaurants and shops, schools and places of worship, and the myriad of commercial and civic buildings that line our historic Main Streets. These buildings—whose charm and conviviality shape the heart of our communities—remind us that, no matter what we design, no matter the region or the style, the timeless values of home and hospitality lie at the heart of what we do. This has carried us a long way, from the back roads of Buckhead, across America, and abroad. May these values, and our cherished clients and friends, stand us in good stead as the journey continues.

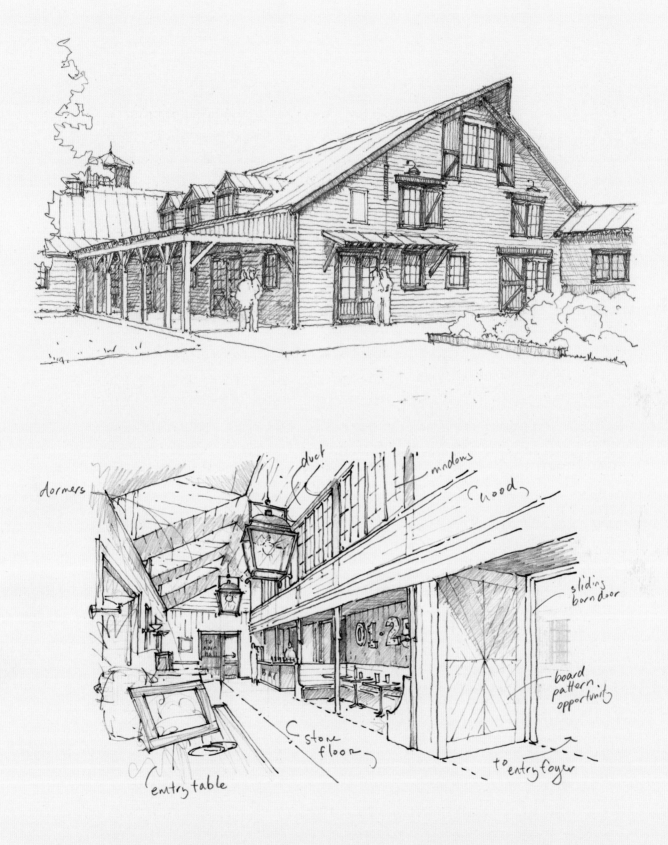

PAGE 220 AND ABOVE: Conceptual sketches and illustrations inform the design of our planning projects and non-residential architecture. By practicing both planning and architecture, we are able to directly connect people to the built environment, thereby extending the idea of "home" to the community at large.

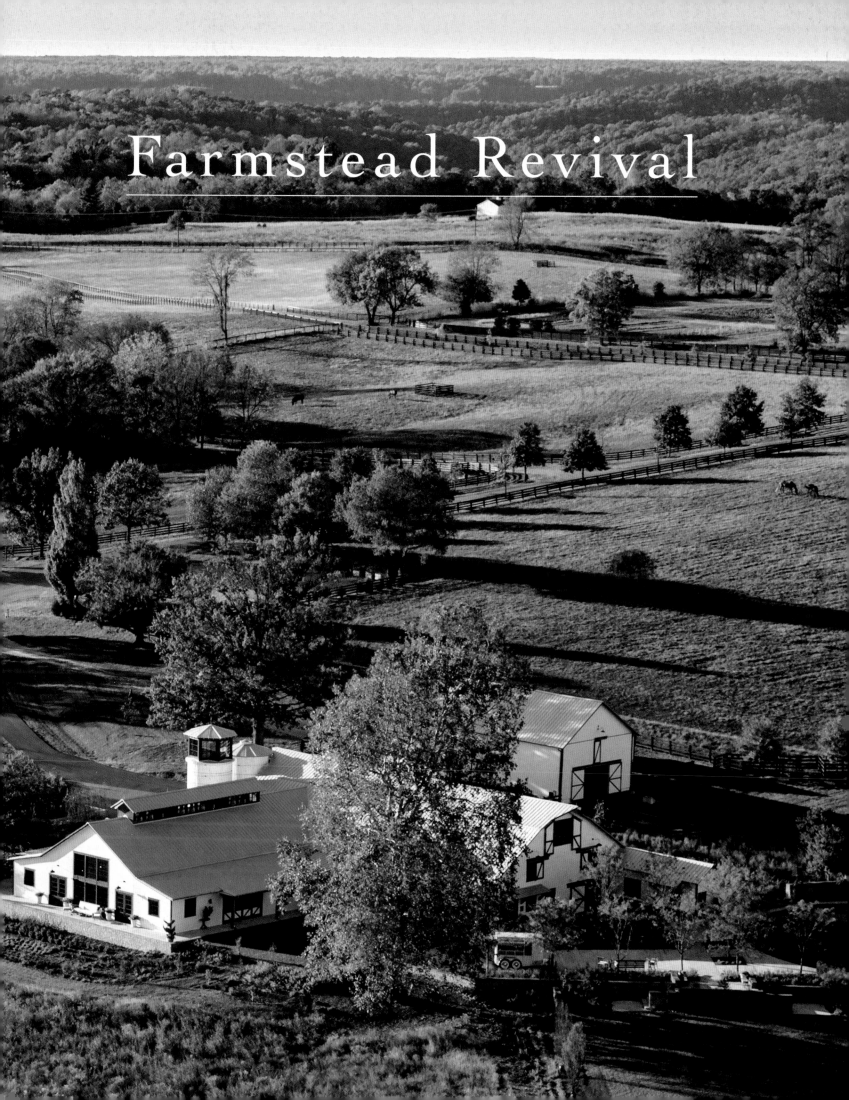

Farmstead Revival

Ashbourne Farms sits in the picturesque rural landscape of La Grange, Kentucky, about forty-five minutes up the Ohio River from Louisville. It is thoroughbred as well as livestock country, and the water flowing through the mineral-rich underground limestone caves is perfect for distilling bourbon. The soil above is no less abundant: its richness and fertility make it ideal for raising the farm-to-table produce for which, along with its poultry and livestock, Ashbourne is justly renowned.

At the heart of the property, and of our project, is the farm's original show barn, once used for viewing and auctioning cattle. This utilitarian building was constructed in the 1930s from dimensioned lumber, with many of the posts holding up the second floor simply built from nailed-together boards. The show barn featured a concrete walkway in the middle, from which potential buyers could consider their bids on the cattle located in the stalls on either side of this provisional promenade. The barn ceased to be active in the late 1960s and had suffered structural deterioration by the time we first visited, its concrete crumbling, its posts and beams sagging and bowed.

Third-generation stewards of the farm, with a deep love for the property and respect for those who preceded them, our clients aspired to restore both the barn and the acreage to their full potential. Focused in equal measure on the beautification, responsible use, and conservation of the land, they enlisted the landscape architecture firm Nelson Byrd Woltz, whose expertise in sustainable agriculture made them the ideal choice. And as a focal point of the master plan, the owners envisioned a beautifully revivified show barn, reconceived as a multifunctional event space.

Our clients recognized that a coat of paint and a new kitchen were not going to transform the building into the world-class facility they had in mind. Apart from cosmetic considerations, a raft of structural and mechanical modifications would be needed to render the project code compliant. But while acknowledging these challenges, they also wanted the finished building to feel authentic. This family understood, and appreciated, the particular character of the old barn—a prime Depression-era example of early Machine Age "agrarian industrial" construction. They wanted, quite simply, to bring the building forward without losing its past. This gave us an exciting and unusual creative challenge, and we warmed to it quickly.

To sustain the connection to history, we kept the straightforward, L-shaped plan of the original building and focused on transforming the procession of spaces as well as their particular uses. On the main floor, a long gallery serves as a welcoming space and includes a bar and sitting area (behind which we set a snug library meant for more intimate get-togethers). Beyond this introduction, in what was the main volume of the barn, lies the skylighted, double-height dining hall (its increased size the sole change to the original footprint). On the second floor, we set a lounge area overlooking the dining hall and, adjacent to it, a music loft designed for concerts showcasing the best in local and regional talent. In addition, each room now frames its own panoramic views of the rolling hills beyond, reminding visitors of what has always been Ashbourne Farms' great attraction and unifying element: the land.

But it was the detailing of the spaces that enabled us to play off, build on, and enhance the barn's original character and draw it into the present day. We worked closely with the project's interior designer, Chenault James, as she developed equestrian and agrarian motifs in brass and leather, and in turn commissioned our frequent collaborator Eloise Pickard to craft custom lighting

PREVIOUS SPREAD: Ashbourne Farms, which has belonged to three generations of the same family, comprises 2,200 arcadian acres in Kentucky. ABOVE: A view of the revivified show barn from the entry court. The converted horse trailer at left, which dispenses cocktails to arriving guests, activates the plaza and lawn, encouraging guests to take in the majestic views of the hills in the distance. RIGHT: A photograph of the barn, snapped in the 1940s, reveals the conviviality and surprisingly formal atmosphere of cattle auction day.

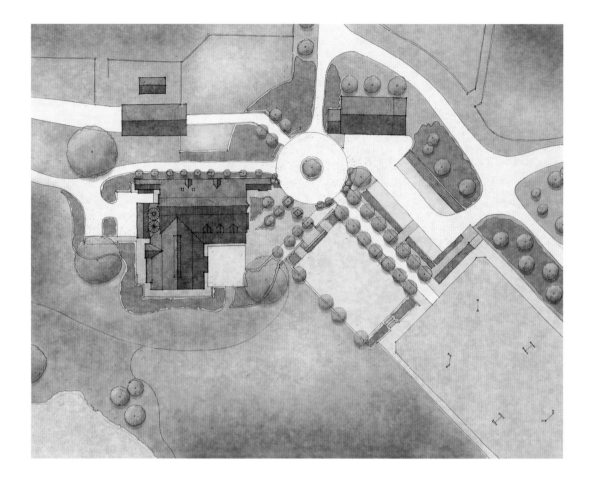

from historic gaslight fixtures and old street lamps. These layers worked seamlessly with the architectural components to convey the show barn's chronological moment. The steel plates, bolted connections, and industrial tensioning elements (in the style of tackle pieces available in the interwar years) let us maximize the structural spans while suggesting improvements that might have been made over the decades. In the end, mixing our industrial interventions with the structure's original elements produced an alternate narrative; one that suggests the building was never dormant and continued to evolve over time. The outcome is entirely fresh yet familiar—at once new and timeless.

Through the course of its renovation, the barn's planned uses unfolded as different opportunities presented themselves. But adding new layers to the story as the design evolved added an authenticity to the building's imagined timeline. We could have taken a strict preservationist approach and frozen the barn in history, or produced an adaptive reuse project that starkly juxtaposed old and new. But either approach would have ignored a compelling fact: all structures transform over time. Understanding how buildings learn is a cornerstone of how we practice—and at Ashbourne Farms, it enabled us to craft a new life for a building that has adapted from generation to generation.

OPPOSITE: Though the show barn has been completely restored, we preserved the vernacular design elements characteristic of the region's prewar utilitarian buildings, including Dutch gables and shed roofs with standing-seam metal cladding; simple wood casing, drop-lap siding, and diagonal braced shutters and barn doors. ABOVE: Surrounded by Ashbourne's equestrian facilities, the show barn is the focal point of an authentic, active horse farm, set in a sublime rural landscape.

ABOVE AND OPPOSITE: On the main floor, the entry gallery includes a bar and casual sitting area. A glance upward reveals the sloped ceiling and dormers. Above the air-conditioning ducts, vintage, overscaled prewar lamps, with their original glass globes, project a full 5 feet from the wall and encourage visitors to imagine the gallery as a village street—warm, welcoming, and infused with the values of a past time.

RIGHT: To the right of the entry gallery, a library doubles as a private lounge that accommodates intimate get-togethers. PAGES 234 AND 235: A secret door in the library's bookcase opens onto a passageway leading to the restrooms. Interior designer Chenault James layered this hideaway and its anterooms with touches of brass, leather, cowhide, and concrete, combining midcentury elements with agrarian and equestrian motifs. The organic palette of creamy white, complementary greens, and warm natural woods carries into the show barn's dining hall.

PREVIOUS SPREAD: We reimagined the barn's expansive main volume as a skylighted double-height dining hall with panoramic views. Here, the original building was expanded in both volume and plan while remaining true to the preexisting proportions and form. ABOVE: A modest service stair adorned with artifacts from Ashbourne Farms' past connects the dining hall and the music loft. OPPOSITE: The bar and lounge area outside the music loft, with slatted walls evoking the architecture of corncribs, overlooks the dining hall below.

In the music loft, which showcases concerts by regional artists, we sought to preserve the look and feel of the original hayloft. Care was taken to preserve as many original elements as possible, but the enhanced space also made room for new features—such as railing balusters crafted from old bourbon barrel staves.

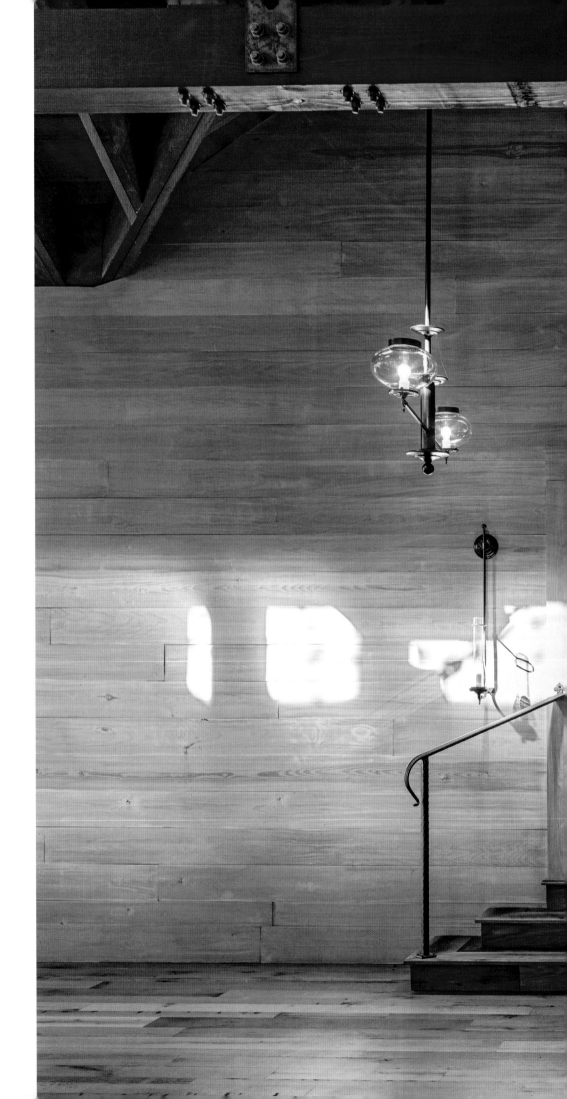

Two original board-formed concrete silos, side by side behind the dining hall, ignited our architectural imaginations, and enabled us to introduce unexpected moments of pure delight. Playfully presented as a choice between door number one and door number two, each silo offers its own unique experience.

ABOVE AND OPPOSITE: Into one of the silos, we inserted a new stair, constructed from wood and gracefully wrapped steel, that serves as a vertical procession between the dining hall and music loft.

ABOVE AND OPPOSITE: The second silo we effectively divided into two spaces. For the lower portion (ABOVE), we created an intimate nook, with an impressionistic mural by Michelle Noe featuring the farm's specific flora and fauna subtly worked into the textured concrete walls. In the upper portion (OPPOSITE), wine racks constructed from reclaimed chestnut rise in a circle, the bottles within reach from a spiral stair with seeded-glass treads that ascend to an observation tower.

ABOVE: The courtyard lawn, accessible from both the dining hall and entry hall, offers an opportunity to take in the splendor of the land. OPPOSITE: The building expresses itself as a collection of pure, ascending agrarian forms. FOLLOWING SPREAD: Ashbourne Farms exemplifies the virtues of preserving what is past while ensuring that it can remain meaningful for generations to come.

PROJECT CREDITS

LOWCOUNTRY GREEK REVIVAL *(pages 2-9)*

HISTORICAL CONCEPTS DESIGN TEAM: Jim Strickland, Clay Rokicki, Mary Elizabeth Bland, Jacques Levet, Jr., David Bryant
CONSTRUCTION: MJR Builders
LANDSCAPE DESIGN: Hooten Land Design
KEY CONTRIBUTORS AND ARTISANS: Eloise Pickard Lighting, Vintage Lumber Sales, Rebecca Godbee, Millwork Artisans, Southern Stair Builders, Melton Classics, New Horizon Shutters, Wood Tectonics, DMG Architectural Specialists

NATURAL HISTORY *(pages 14-39)*

HISTORICAL CONCEPTS DESIGN TEAM: Jim Strickland, Terry Pylant, Ryan Yurcaba, Camden McClelland, Paul Haislmaier
CONSTRUCTION: Terry Hoff Construction
INTERIOR DESIGN: Westbrook Interiors
LANDSCAPE DESIGN: Hooten Land Design
KEY CONTRIBUTORS AND ARTISANS: Vintage Lumber Sales, Tree Marsh Woodworks, Millwork Artisans, Bob Christian Decorative Art, Rheinzink, Charleston Plaster Co., Woolen Mill Fan Company, DMG Architectural Specialists, Architectural Accents, Stewart Brannen Millworks, Berlin G. Myers Lumber Corp., William C. Pritchard Co., Old Carolina Brick Co., New Horizon Shutters, Waterworks, Carolina Lanterns, Rose Tarlow, Hector Finch

RAMBLING WEST *(pages 40-59)*

HISTORICAL CONCEPTS DESIGN TEAM: Jim Strickland, Aaron Daily, J.P. Curran, David Bryant, Jessi Rokicki
CONSTRUCTION: Lee Gilman Builders
LANDSCAPE DESIGN: Hooten Land Design and Eggers Associates
KEY CONTRIBUTORS AND ARTISANS: Eloise Pickard Lighting, Martine Drackett, Bend River Windows & Doors, Ketchum Custom Woodworks, Ben Gilman, Rolling Rock Building Stone, Ball and Ball Hardware, Liv Jensen, P.E.

RESTORED RETREAT *(pages 64-85)*

HISTORICAL CONCEPTS DESIGN TEAM: Andrew Cogar, Elizabeth Dillon, Rebecca Pendley, David VanGroningen, Colleen O'Keeffe
CONSTRUCTION: T&S Mott
INTERIOR DESIGN: S.R. Gambrel, Inc.
LANDSCAPE DESIGN: Hollander Design and Marders
KEY CONTRIBUTORS AND ARTISANS: Little Harbor Window Co., Michael M. Coldren Co., Carpen House, Smith River Kitchens, Upstate Door, Heritage Wide Plank Flooring, Timberlane, Hampton Glass & Mirror, Wm. J. Mills & Co., Sunrise Specialty, Schoolhouse Electric, Remains Lighting, Alan T. Brady, P.E., 2RW

SEASIDE ENSEMBLE *(pages 86-105)*

HISTORICAL CONCEPTS DESIGN TEAM: Andrew Cogar, Elizabeth Dillon, David VanGroningen, Colleen O'Keeffe, Rebecca Pendley
CONSTRUCTION: Bulgin & Associates
INTERIOR DESIGN: S.R. Gambrel, Inc.
LANDSCAPE DESIGN: Nelson Byrd Woltz Landscape Architects
KEY CONTRIBUTORS AND ARTISANS: Reilly Architectural, Baba Antique Wooden Floors, Rising Sun Woodworking, Archive Designs, Michael M. Coldren Co., Frank Allart & Co., Architectural Accents, Upstate Door, Timberlane, Lido Stone Works, Waterworks, The Urban Electric Co., Jamb, Alan T. Brady, P.E.

THE DOWAGER INN *(pages 106-135)*

HISTORICAL CONCEPTS DESIGN TEAM: Andrew Cogar, Elizabeth Dillon, Chris Eiland,
Lora Shea, Kellen Krause
CONSTRUCTION: Timeless Homes Ltd.
INTERIOR DESIGN: Bryan Graybill
LANDSCAPE DESIGN: Hooten Land Design
KEY CONTRIBUTORS AND ARTISANS: William Suchite, Eiland Woodworks, Ronnie Nettles,
D&A Binder, Paul Clifford, Millwork Artisans, Vintage Lumber Sales, Jamb,
Michael M. Coldren Co., Upstate Door, Waterworks, Catchpole & Rye, Drummonds,
Woka Lamps Vienna, Roman and Williams Guild, Savvy Stoneworks, ABC Stone,
Lepage Millwork, DMG Architectural Specialists

THE SIMPLE LIFE *(pages 140-161)*

HISTORICAL CONCEPTS DESIGN TEAM: Kevin Clark, Colleen O'Keeffe, Rene Salas,
Paul Knight, Claire Smith
CONSTRUCTION: Simpson Construction
INTERIOR DESIGN: Havilande Whitcomb Design
LANDSCAPE DESIGN: Hooten Land Design
KEY CONTRIBUTORS AND ARTISANS: Burchette and Burchette Hardwood, Old Carolina
Brick Co., New Horizon Shutters, Vintage Lumber Sales, Kolbe Windows, Boral Siding,
Portella Steel Doors & Windows, Bevolo Gas & Electric Lights, Mark of Excellence
Custom Woodworking, Rick Young, TruStile Doors, The Kayan Group

PRECEDENT REDEFINED *(pages 162-189)*

HISTORICAL CONCEPTS DESIGN TEAM: Jim Strickland, Clay Rokicki, Forest Sickles,
Daniel Osborne
CONSTRUCTION: Koenig Construction
INTERIOR DESIGN: Amanda Nisbet Design
LANDSCAPE DESIGN: Laurie Durden Garden Design
KEY CONTRIBUTORS AND ARTISANS: Brombal, Robert Thomas Iron Design,
Gray Bell Millwork, Burchette and Burchette Hardwood, MW Millworks,
Remains Lighting, The Urban Electric Co., Soane Britain, Millwork Artisans,
Simeon A. Warren, Vintage Lumber Sales, Aqua Blue Pools

IT TAKES A VILLAGE *(pages 190-219)*

HISTORICAL CONCEPTS DESIGN TEAM: Andrew Cogar, Elizabeth Dillon, Jessi Rokicki,
Lora Shea, Kellen Krause
CONSTRUCTION: Seascape Partners
INTERIOR DESIGN: S.R. Gambrel, Inc.
LANDSCAPE DESIGN: Soil, Inc.
KEY CONTRIBUTORS AND ARTISANS: Lance Nils, Michael M. Coldren Co.,
A+ Painting, Lido Stone Works, Bradley, The Urban Electric Co., Hector Finch,
Archive Designs, Reilly Architectural, Waterworks, Hyde Park Mouldings,
Reither Woodworking, DMG Architectural Specialists, Alan T. Brady, P.E.

FARMSTEAD REVIVAL *(pages 224-251)*

HISTORICAL CONCEPTS DESIGN TEAM: Domenick Treschitta, Allyson Vincent, Daniel Osborne,
Ryan Yurcaba
CONSTRUCTION: Realm Construction Company
INTERIOR DESIGN: Chenault James Interiors
LANDSCAPE DESIGN: Nelson Byrd Woltz Landscape Architects
KEY CONTRIBUTORS AND ARTISANS: Eloise Pickard Lighting, Rodney Wedge, Gray Wilson
Furniture, Four Board Woodworks, Pioneer Log Systems, Sentry Steel, Skylight Supply,
H&D Brass, Ancient Surfaces, C.G. King, Salter Spiral Stair, Maynard Studios,
Architectural Accents, Molnar Jordan & Associates, Starzer Brady Fagan Associates,
Engineered Lighting Sales, Spectrum Sight & Sound

ACKNOWLEDGMENTS

Since taking the helm at Historical Concepts, I have had the pleasure of following in the footsteps of our founder, James Strickland. He has been an inspiration, a mentor, and a friend. From my very first day, I have witnessed as Jim put in place a dream of what our firm could be when we remained dedicated to our clients, and to each other, through common design principles and values. And I have been fortunate to stand on the shoulders of giants—my partners and peers Todd Strickland, Terry Pylant, Aaron Daily, Kevin Clark, Domenick Treschitta, Elizabeth Dillon, Kristy Tindall, Clay Rokicki, and David VanGroningen. My partners are the sources of creativity and inspiration that drive the success of our firm, each in his or her own way representing the example of excellence set by Jim.

In the process of writing this book, I had the privilege of engaging with every member of our staff, where they reaffirmed our common commitment to create enduring beauty and improve the lives of our clients and our communities. I am deeply grateful for their daily dedication and commitment. They are Connor Bingham, Mary Elizabeth Bland, David Bryant, Christopher Carrigan, Leslie Daily, Chris Eiland, Ian Griffey, Paul Haislmaier, Allison Hora, Paul Knight, Kellen Krause, Lindsay LaBudde, Camden McClelland, Ashley Morrison, Colleen O'Keeffe, Laurie Pate, Rebecca Pendley, Jessi Rokicki, Rene Salas, Matt Schaefer, Andrew Seago, Maddie Seago, Lora Shea, Forest Sickles, Andrea Steck, Lucas Stegeman, Ginny Stern, Suzanne Stern, Laura Strickland, Linda Strickland, Allyson Vincent, and Ryan Yurcaba. These individuals are, quite simply, the heart and soul of Historical Concepts. And, I am especially grateful to Dawn Fritz, our marketing manager, who has efficiently guided the process of putting this book together while cultivating the creative input of all those involved.

I would be remiss if I did not also acknowledge the work of former principal Daniel Osborne and past associates J.P. Curran, Christy Dodson, Sandra Guritz, Jacques Levet, Jr., Nina Meyer Cox, Liza Mueller, Anne Marie Noll, Becky Sigman, Claire Smith, Megan Sommers, Amy Trum, and Geoff Yovanovic. A most heartfelt thank-you to one and all.

It took a seasoned group of experts to write, design, publish, and promote this book. We were fortunate to again have the support of Charles Miers and Sandy Gilbert Freidus at Rizzoli International Publications, Inc. Tom Maciag and his team of web/graphic designers at Dyad Communications have helped us tell our story digitally since the publication of our first book, *Coming Home*. Sarah Burningham of Little Bird Publicity has guided us from the onset of *Visions of Home* and remains a trusted counselor and friend. Marc Kristal's superb writing is matched only by his wit; his ability to listen and question brought out the true story I wanted to tell. And the dynamic duo of photographer Eric Piasecki and stylist Helen Crowther produced images beyond our wildest dreams; their ability to read both my mind and the architecture is uncanny. Book designers Doug Turshen and David Huang wove the photography with our story into a compelling visual narrative that showcases our work in ways beyond our hopes and expectations. And last but certainly not least, a special thanks to our agent Jill Cohen, whose impeccable eye, sensitive understanding of our reader, and unwavering ability to tell us what we needed to hear has been invaluable.

Our work would not be what it is without the countless builders, artisans, designers, landscape architects, and engineers with whom we collaborate every day. Thank you for your passion, craftsmanship, and professionalism. We learn from all of you with each new project.

I would like to thank my wife, Amanda, and daughter, Edie Belle, who give me the love, support, and motivation to be the best person I can be. I would also like to thank my parents for instilling in me a sense of service and kindness to others, along with demonstrating a work ethic and deep intellectual curiosity that has been the basis of my career. A heartfelt thanks to the educators who opened my eyes to the art, science, and responsibility of architecture: formative teachers Earle Holt, James F. White, Donald J. McNamara, and professors at the University of Miami, including Rocco Ceo, Denis Hector, Roberto Behar, Joanna Lombard, and former dean Elizabeth Plater-Zyberk. And a sincere thanks to Steven Gambrel, Barbara Sallick, Elizabeth Dowling, Mark Ferguson, Tim Barber, Michael Mesko, Bill Harrison, Russell Windham, Peter Lyden, and the many other friends, collaborators, and kindred spirits with the Institute of Classical Art & Architecture.

In closing, there are simply not enough words to convey my deep sense of gratitude to our clients. Each of you has entrusted us with your dreams and, in our close work together, your dreams have become ours. We are forever grateful for your generosity of spirit and faith in our talent and craft. Thank you for making this book possible.

THE PARTNERS OF HISTORICAL CONCEPTS: Seated (left to right): Todd Strickland, James L. Strickland (Founder), Kristy Tindall, Andrew Cogar (President), and Aaron Daily. Standing (left to right): David VanGroningen, Kevin Clark, Elizabeth Dillon, Terry Pylant, Clay Rokicki, and Domenick Treschitta.

First published in the United States of America in 2021 by
Rizzoli International Publications, Inc.
300 Park Avenue South
New York, NY 10010
www.rizzoliusa.com

© 2021 Historical Concepts
All photography by Eric Piasecki, with the exception of pages 73 and 76
(bottom, left) by Douglas Friedman, and page 255 by David Christensen
Publisher: Charles Miers
Project Editor: Sandra Gilbert Freidus
General Editor: Dawn Fritz
Editorial Assistance: Hilary Ney, Stephanie Salomon, Rachel Selekman
Design: Doug Turshen with David Huang
Production Manager: Kaija Markoe
Managing Editor: Lynn Scrabis

Printed in China

2021 2022 2023 2024 / 10 9 8 7 6 5 4 3 2 1

ISBN: 978-0-8478-6760-8
Library of Congress Control Number: 2020948902

Visit us online:
Facebook.com/RizzoliNewYork
instagram.com/rizzolibooks
twitter.com/Rizzoli_Books
pinterest.com/rizzolibooks
youtube.com/user/RizzoliNY
issuu.com/Rizzoli